WEIRD FACTS
ABOUT
TORONTO

A.H. Ja

BLUE
BIKE
BOOKS

The Publisher: Blue Bike Books
Website: www.bluebikebooks.com

Library and Archives Canada Cataloguing in Publication

Jackson, A.H., 1944–
    Weird facts about Toronto / A.H. Jackson.

ISBN 978-1-926700-09-0

    1. Toronto (Ont.)—Miscellanea. I. Title.

FC3097.3.J33 2011   971.3'541   C2010-907628-1

Project Director: Nicholle Carrière
Project Editor: Wendy Pirk
Cover Image: Royal Ontario Museum, © Scott Norsworthy
Illustrations: Roger Garcia, Peter Tyler, Roly Wood, Pat Bidwell, Patrick Hénaff

We acknowledge the support of the Alberta Foundation for the Arts for our
publishing program.

We acknowledge the financial support of the Government of Canada through
the Canada Book Fund (CBF) for our publishing activities.

Canadian Heritage   Patrimoine canadien

PC: 5

DEDICATION

*This one is for Dana B. and Eric,
the Duke and Duchess of Lynwood*

CONTENTS

ACKNOWLEDGEMENTS

Kudos to the men and women of Toronto's Public Library, Archives and Works Department who turned ferreting out the "weird" from a metropolis most noted for its invention of Pablum a less daunting task. Mining weird facts requires reams of information that the Toronto Public Library, especially the Deer Park branch, never fails to deliver in a timely fashion. Big thanks to the Toronto Archives for being a steadfast depositary of all things historical including the weird, and to the Toronto Works Department for ignoring my poking about in their odd collection of lost streams and rivers.

Big thanks to the folks at Blue Bike Books, especially to my editor Wendy Pirk, who picks up my every error and never complains.

City Timeline

I have very happy memories of fairy tales. My mother used to take me to the library in Toronto to check out the fairy tales. And she was an actress, so she used to act out for me the different characters in all these fairy tales.

–Mike Myers, actor

A SHORT HISTORY OF TORONTO

1750: French fur traders led by the Marquis de la Jonquière build a small trading post at the mouth of the Humber River that they called Fort Rouillé.

1755: Fort Rouillé receives a small garrison of French soldiers for protection, along with a few families of settlers to grow food.

1758: With French-controlled Fort Niagara about to fall to the British and unwilling to let Fort Rouillé fall into enemy hands, the French burn it to the ground. Today, visitors to the Canadian National Exhibition, or CNE, are able to walk the grounds of where it all began because a stone obelisk marks the spot where Fort Rouillé once guarded the Humber River and controlled access to the interior.

1787: Through a legal treaty called The Toronto Purchase, the British Crown establishes title to over 100,000 hectares of land bordering Lake Ontario for the construction of the new capital of Canada West to be called Toronto, or Terento, depending on what surveyor was working the plans. The vendors, the Mississauga band of First Nations peoples, accept a few hundred pounds, 2000 gun flints, two dozen each of kettles and hats, all the hand mirrors they can carry and 380 litres of excellent navy rum.

1793: Governor Simcoe changes the settlement's name of "Toronto" to "York" in honour of the King's second son, Frederick Augustus, Duke of York's great European military victory over the French at Flanders.

1797: Toronto is now called York, but farther up Lake Ontario, 109 kilometres to the east, there exists a newly incorporated village that was named Smith's Falls by its founder but is called Toronto by residents who prefer the name abandoned by the capital.

1803: The area at King and Jarvis Streets is designated as a market block for the sale of produce, meat, cheese and other goods, and becomes a bustling centre of commerce.

1808: A lighthouse constructed on Gibraltar Point at the western tip of the sandspit peninsula protecting Toronto Harbour beams a guiding light into the darkness over Lake Ontario. Called the Gibraltar Point Lighthouse, the stone structure survives to this day and is Toronto's oldest surviving building.

1812: On June 18, America declares war on Britain, but York's citizens are not overly concerned as British troops and the city's fortifications seem adequate for protection.

1813: The American invasion of York gets underway on the afternoon of April 27, when 14 American ships carrying Brigadier General Zebulon Pike and 1700 U.S. soldiers find their primary target of Burlington too heavily defended and revert to Plan B, an invasion of York. Under attack by superior forces, Fort York's garrison retreats while setting fire to several ships under construction along with the fort's substantial powder magazine. The explosion of the magazine kills General Pike and 32 soldiers and wounds 222, an action that so infuriates the invaders, they burn the government buildings and loot homes of government officials.

1814: The American fleet returns for another try at taking the city but find that the British have constructed a new and better Fort York, so the Americans are unable to land their invasion force. The disgruntled invaders burn the blockhouse at Gibraltar Point and make off with a herd of goats.

1817: At Smith's Falls, the sign over the newly erected village post office reads "Smith's Falls," but at the town limits, a sign reads "Toronto," as does every other sign in town, along with the official government stamp in the lawyer's office.

1819: Although mail comes addressed to Smith's Falls, the daily stagecoach arrives and departs from Toronto, as do all official documents because the government registrar of deeds has the good people of Smith's Falls living in Toronto. Growing tired of the name confusion and misdirected mail, local residents decide at their annual New Year's town meeting to change the village name to that of their cemetery, Port Hope. Their decision is cause for celebration in York, as citizens there have grown tired of the monikers "Muddy York" and "Little York" and of having their mail go to a dozen other places named York.

1830: The market block at King and Jarvis is razed by fire.

1831: Rebuilt in brick, a corner building of the market block at King and Jarvis becomes Toronto's first city hall.

1833: The city's three access roads—Young Street, Dundas Street and Kingston Road—are in such bad condition that the legislature is forced to allot money to have them macadamized, a gravel-road building technique developed in 1820 by Scotsman John Loudon McAdam. While Young and Dundas Streets are repaired using McAdam's technique, the Kingston Road project uses wood planks to reduce cost.

City officials, concerned about the way waterfront industry is infilling the lake to create land, set a lakeshore boundary by drawing a line across the harbour map from James Wort's windmill to the site of old Fort Rouillé, calling it the Windmill Line.

1834: A session of the Ontario legislature officially reinstates the name "Toronto" to the city of York and recognizes the newly incorporated town of Port Hope.

A cholera epidemic kills 20 percent of Toronto's residents.

1837: Insurrection makes for thirsty participants, so where better to begin a revolt than a tavern? Montgomery's Tavern, on Yonge Street north of York, is the spot that former Toronto mayor William Lyon Mackenzie picks to overturn the government by launching a raid on the armoury at York. British troops have gone east to help put down a rebellion in Lower Canada, leaving York lightly defended by militia. Mackenzie's big chance arrives, but he lingers over too many beers, allowing time for reinforcements with cannons to arrive from Hamilton. Forced back to the tavern, Mackenzie and his half-drunk rebel forces hightail it, leaving the tavern to be sacked of its liquid contents and burned to the ground by the victorious defenders of York.

1838: The city constructs its first sanitary sewer line, along King Street from York to Berkley Street, with half the cost charged to residents on both sides of King at a rate of 5 shillings per foot (30 centimetres) of frontage. The sewer dumps its foul contents into Toronto Bay at the foot of York Street.

1842: Gas lighting installed on Toronto's main streets by Albert Furniss' Toronto Gaslight and Water Company so impresses a visiting Charles Dickens that he writes the following to a friend: "The town itself is full of life and motion, bustle, business and improvement. The streets are well paved and lighted with gas; the houses are large and good, the shops excellent."

1843: Lake boat owner Captain Thomas Dick buys a row of houses on Front near York Street and cobbles them into a hotel he names the Ontario Terrace.

1844: Publisher George Brown establishes the *Globe* newspaper, precursor to the modern *Globe and Mail*, as a political vehicle to benefit Toronto's Reformist movement.

1846: The Toronto Incorporations Act is amended to create a Recorders Court, enabling the city to pass bylaws and collect fines for infractions. While most bylaws deal with fire prevention, one allows the city to charge owners of property with indoor plumbing an annual rental fee for drains connected to city sewers.

1847: As many as 40,000 Irish immigrants fleeing the effects of the Great Famine arrive in the city during the summer months, bringing cholera and typhus fever. Healthy immigrants are sent out of the city, while those exhibiting symptoms of the disease are sent to the fever sheds and allowed to stay for six days. Almost 900 succumb to the illness, with victims buried in mass graves at St. Paul's Catholic Church at Queen and Power Streets and the General Burying Grounds at Yorkville.

1849: Toronto's first Great Fire begins in the city core, at Post's Tavern, and spreads to engulf the entire business section, including city hall.

1850: A new city hall is built in a grander style.

1852: A violent storm smashes into the great sandspit that protects Toronto Harbour, breaching a channel in a narrow strip at the eastern end called Fisherman's Island. This sandy strip connected to the mainland past Ashbridges Bay is vulnerable to the storm because of people removing sand for construction purposes.

1853: Captain Dick partners with Patrick Sword to refurbish the Ontario Terrace Hotel, and they rename it the Sword Hotel. The Northern Railway constructs a railway depot on Front Street, near the site of today's Union Station, from where the first trains arrive and depart from Toronto.

1855: Under new ownership, the Sword Hotel is once again renovated and renamed the Revere Hotel.

The bell tower in Port Hope is constructed, and though the clock keeps perfect time, it runs a half-hour slow, a mechanical glitch impossible to rectify. No problem, because a half-hour late is fine with locals, until 1876 when Peterborough resident Sir Stanford Fleming invents "standard time" after a misprint on a steamship schedule causes him to miss a trip to Ireland.

The infilled lakeshore known as the Esplanade is lengthened for a pathway and parks, but instead attracts factories, iron foundries and shipping wharves.

1858: On April 13, a violent storm widens the eastern channel into a 90-metre-wide gap, washing away the newly remodelled Quinn's Hotel scheduled to open the following day. The storm leaves the peninsula looking like Swiss cheese, turning it into a chain of genuine islands. The largest, comprising most of the old peninsula, is Centre Island; the four smaller inshore islands are named Muggs, Algonquin, Middle and Olympic Islands; and the three tiny, interior islands are called Forestry, Snake and South Islands. Another, mistakenly called Ward's Island, is actually part of Centre Island.

The first Union Station, a large, lead-covered shed shared by both the Northern and the Great Western Railway, is built on York Street.

1859: The city establishes a new police force with constables hired and supervised by a commission. Police constables are banned from owning taverns, and membership in the Orange Order is frowned upon. However, most of the 22 constables rehired from the old force are Orangemen with ownership of their taverns transferred to relatives.

1860: Toronto's citizens get a glimpse of future "minder" attitudes of their new Board of Commissioners of Police with the passing of Bylaw 322, which outlaws snowball throwing in city parks.

1861: The American Civil War begins and has a profound polarizing effect on the city with both sides in the conflict having local sympathizers. The southern Confederacy enjoys so much support that during the war's final years, the Queen's Hotel on Front Street becomes the South's de facto headquarters.

1862: Captain Dick repurchases the Revere Hotel, and after extensive renovations and additions, he renames his now-stately edifice the Queen's Hotel, the precursor to the modern-day Fairmont Royal York Hotel.

1867: The Crown grants ownership of the Toronto Islands to the city, which begins to lease out lots for cottage construction.

1873: The Northern Railway constructs a larger facility, the second Union Station, on the northeast corner of Simcoe Street and the Esplanade.

1874: Hanlan's Hotel, constructed by John Hanlan, father of world champion rower Ned Hanlan, opens in the area known today as Hanlan's Point.

1878: Toronto hosts the Provincial Agricultural Fair, an exhibition staged in different Ontario cities each fall. The event attracts over 100,000 visitors and is so successful that the city lobbies the province for permanency.

1879: Toronto holds its first Toronto Industrial Exhibition on the Garrison Common of Fort York, a site now occupied by the Canadian National Exhibition (CNE), a name change implemented to reflect the national spirit. Over the years, the CNE will serve as a showcase venue for advances in industrial technology.

Under licence from the Bell family, Hugh Cossart Baker Jr. builds the British Empire's first telephone exchange in Hamilton, Ontario, and strings wire into Toronto. By the end of the year, Toronto has so many telephones that

Baker helpfully publishes a list of subscribers, Toronto's first telephone book.

1880: Baker receives a charter to build a national telephone company, the Hamilton Telephone Company, precursor to the giant Bell Canada.

Ned Hanlan opens the new Hotel Hanlan and includes a small amusement park for patrons that will be the catalyst for the fabulous Hanlan's Point Amusement Park.

A conservative syndicate headed by Senator Robert Jaffray buys the *Globe*.

1884: J.J. Wright demonstrates the electric-motor-powered railcar at the CNE.

1889: City hall and its appendage market stalls undergo renovations, including the addition of the huge roof that survives to this day.

1892: The *Evening Star* newspaper, precursor to the modern-day *Toronto Star,* is published by a group of printers locked out by another newspaper, the *Toronto News.*

1894: A dredging and reclamation project by the Toronto Ferry Company creates land on the area of the Toronto Islands called Hanlan's Point for a park that will expand into a massive boardwalk of amusement rides and food concessions called Hanlan's Point Amusement Park.

1895: City police get their first boat, allowing them to patrol beaches and apprehend bathers wearing swimsuits deemed inappropriate.

1896: East end Toronto gets a place to escape the summer heat when the Toronto Railway Company (TRC) opens Munro Park, the first of its three "trolley park" family entertainment complexes in The Beaches area of the city.

1899: The city government abandons its offices in the Market Square building for the new city hall constructed at Bay and Queen Streets.

The *Evening Star* is purchased as a media political tool by a group of Toronto Reformists to counter the right-wing political influence of the *Toronto Globe*. The paper is put into the hands of former *Globe* reporter Joseph E. Atkinson, who eventually achieves controlling interest in what is dubbed "a paper for the people."

1903: U.S. industrialist Andrew Carnegie gives the city a total of $487,500 (about $20 million in today's money) for the construction of library extensions. There is an effort by labour unions to refuse the grants, but clearer heads on city council prevail.

1904: Toronto's second Great Fire begins on Wellington Street at the E&S Currie necktie factory on the cold and blustery evening of April 19. In spite of massive firefighter response, the fire quickly progresses to engulf the entire business section, destroying more than 100 buildings and leaving 5000 citizens out of work.

1906: Two brothers, Jule and Jay Allen, open the city's first permanent movie theatre, the Theatorium, at 183 Yonge Street. Later called the Red Mill, the movie house is the second star in the Allen's movie-theatre empire that will grow to more than 100 theatres cross Canada.

1907: The Scarboro Amusement Park opens in The Beaches area between McLean and Leuty Avenues, and Torontonians get their first taste of Coney Island–style thrills.

1911: The Arena Gardens, later renamed the Mutual Street Arena, is constructed, giving the city its first artificial-ice venue for skating, curling and hockey.

1914: The Great War in Europe ultimately kills 10,000 Toronto volunteers, with four times that many returning maimed and wounded. On the home front, rationing goes into effect with resident families entitled to purchase only 1.8 kilograms of meat, 220 grams of sugar and 26 litres of gasoline weekly.

On September 5, baseball great Babe Ruth smacks the first homer of his professional career out of Hanlan's Point Stadium into the bay.

The Toronto Blueshirts win the Stanley Cup at the Arena Gardens.

1916: The Ontario Temperance Act leaves the city high, dry and thirsty, but because a loophole allows doctors to prescribe whisky and brandy, almost every city pharmacy installs a soda fountain to supply ice, mix and a nice place for prescribees to imbibe...*hic!*

1918: The Spanish flu ravages the city, claiming between 1200 and 1500 lives in two waves.

The Torontos, the first National Hockey Association franchise, win the Stanley Cup.

1921: The Toronto Transportation Commission (TTC) is established through the merger of the privately owned Toronto Street Railway with the city-owned Toronto Civic Railway.

1922: Sunnyside Amusement Park opens as an adjunct to the Toronto Harbour Commission's newly constructed beach-bathing pavilion and 4 kilometres of boardwalk.

The Toronto St. Pats (renamed the Maple Leafs in 1927) take the Stanley Cup.

1923: Foster Hewitt broadcasts the first hockey game from the Mutual Street Arena.

1926: The world's largest swimming pool opens at Sunnyside Amusement Park.

The Great Motherhood Race proposed in the last will and testament of wealthy land speculator and lawyer Charles Vance Millar gets underway and galvanizes the city for 10 years. Millar's reward to the mother who births the most children in a 10-year period is $100,000 in company shares. At the end, four women share the reward, each having given birth to nine children...*Whaaa!*

1927: The current and third Union Station opens on land acquired by the city after the Great Fire of 1904.

The Ontario Temperance Act is repealed through referendum, only to be replaced by a draconian liquor-rationing system, the infamous LCBO, and the city gets its first provincially run liquor store.

In July, the federally run Toronto Terminals Railway Company opens its new Union Station to the public.

1929: The Great Depression spreads into Toronto from the U.S. like a disease. The stock market crashes, industry grinds to a halt, unemployment soars and soup lines form.

1931: The iconic arena of the National Hockey League, Maple Leaf Gardens opens on November 12, with the home team Maple Leafs losing 2–1 to the Chicago Black Hawks.

Thanks to the Great Depression, over 20 percent of Toronto's workers are unemployed.

1932: Thirty percent of Toronto's workers are now out of work with soup lines stretching around city blocks. Immigrants without jobs risk deportation, while thousands of homeless men shuffle off to federal work camps.

1933: A friendly ball game at Christie Pits Playground between the all-Jewish Harbord Playground team and the St. Peter's

Church team turns ugly after a group of taunting Nazi sympathizers unfurls a swastika-inscribed bedsheet. Enraged, the Jewish team charges the Nazi sympathizers and the fight is on. The conflict is small at first, but when each side calls in reinforcements what transpires is a full-blown riot that lasts six hours. The riot features cracked heads, broken ribs, noses and teeth but no loss of life. When the dust settles, the Jewish team leaves the area feeling proud of having stood up to ingrained anti-Semitism. Over the years, the Christie Pits Riot has become urban legend with as many as 10,000 participants, but the reality is more like 300 rioters with perhaps 1000 spectators.

1936: The Jaffray family loses control of the *Globe* when the paper merges with the *Mail and Empire* newspaper and is renamed the *Globe and Mail*.

1938: City government begins its long and insidious campaign to steal the lakeshore from its citizens when it expropriates the west end of the Toronto Islands for the construction of the Island Airport.

1942: The Glenn Miller Band performs at the Mutual Street Arena to a standing-room-only crowd of over 6000.

1949: The SS *Noronic* burns in Toronto Harbour, killing 118 passengers.

1952: Metro Toronto is created by the amalgamation of all hamlets, villages and towns in a geographical area bounded by Etobicoke Creek on the west, the Rouge River on the east and Steeles Avenue on the north.

1954: The Yonge Street subway goes into operation on March 30 between Union Station and Eglinton Avenue, with stops in between.

On October 15, Hurricane Hazel flattens the city and floods the lower sections of the subway.

1961: The Don Valley Parkway opens, and a search by concerned citizens for the idiot who designed an expressway with few shoulders and an unusable lane proves fruitless as city council refuses to divulge the name of the individual.

1965: The Big Blackout plunges the city into darkness on November 9, at 5:16 PM, during the height of rush hour. Although the lights go back on in three to four hours, the chaos those hours of total blackness create is astounding. To this day, the exact cause of the blackout is undetermined, but many blame UFOs, as many sightings are reported around the Niagara Falls generating station.

1967: The Toronto Maple Leafs win the Stanley Cup, apparently for the last time.

1999: The Waterfront Revitalization Corporation, also known as Waterfront Toronto, a partnership of federal, provincial and city governments, replaces the Toronto Harbour Commission to oversee reconstruction of the waterfront.

1970: The Harbour City plan, a Venice-style canal treatment for the waterfront, creates much excitement but goes nowhere thanks to federal, provincial and city bickering.

1971: Ontario Place, the sole survivor of the Harbour City plan, is constructed.

The construction of the Spadina Expressway is cancelled as a result of widespread opposition by citizens. A few infuriated city councillors seek revenge by voting for a rise in property taxes and squandering the proceeds.

1976: The CN Tower opens and interference with radio and television transmissions by tall buildings is no longer a concern.

1992: The Toronto Blue Jays trump the Atlanta Braves on their home turf to win the World Series.

1993: The Blue Jays defeat the Philadelphia Phillies at the Skydome, now called the Rogers Centre.

1998: The cities of East York, Etobicoke, Scarborough, North York and York are amalgamated into the new City of Toronto.

2000: The city purchases Union Station from the federally operated Toronto Terminals Railway Company Limited, while provincially owned Go Transit buys the tracks.

2003: The Great Northeast Blackout cuts power to the city on August 14, at 4:11 PM, for the entire night. With sirens wailing in the background, city residents fire up their barbeques and dine by candlelight while hundreds are stranded in elevators and subway cars and await rescue.

2005: A Boxing Day gang shooting on Yonge Street kills innocent bystander Jane Creba and wounds six others.

On June 2, authorities announce the arrest of the Toronto 18, an Islamic terrorist group bent on mass destruction to the city and its residents.

2010: The G20 summit held at the Toronto Convention Centre becomes an iconic fiasco of overreaction by police services and unfettered spending by politicians.

INTRODUCTION

Out of the Wilderness

In the beginning, there was only malarial swamp, oak forest and a river the Iroquois called Tkaronto, now called the Humber River. French explorers happened upon the area by following the heavy traffic of First Nations peoples. This was their way to the north country; when French fur traders came along, the route was known as the Taranteau Passage until the arrival of the British in 1791, when it became Toronto or Torento Passage, depending on the engineer working the plans for the temporary settlement. Newark, also known as Niagara-by-the-Beach, and today Niagara-on-the-Lake, had been the seat of government for Upper Canada, but Lieutenant-Governor John Graves Simcoe deemed it indefensible against American forces and instituted a move. Toronto, with its excellent natural harbour, was well out of reach of American guns, and the passage north offered a quick way out of town if the Americans should invade. Toronto was to be a temporary seat of government until a road west could be built through the Queen's bush (they did call it that) to a location that Governor Simcoe had deemed more appropriate for area defence, a place to be called "London" as a tribute to his home city in England.

Governor Simcoe was a military man ill suited for the compromise of politics, and though his career suffered from his military-style edicts, his four-and-a-half-year tenure prepared the province for impending conflict with the U.S. In a military fashion, Simcoe laid out Toronto's town centre and road system in equidistant blocks and straight-line roads around a freshwater spring. To allow for retreat from American invaders, Simcoe chose a First Nations trail north that he called Yonge Street, after the British Secretary of War, Sir George Yonge.

Simcoe also drew a horizontal line on his map where civilization stopped and the wilderness began, calling it Lot Street. Renamed Queen Street in 1837 to honour Queen Victoria's ascension to the English throne, Lot Street was the hook that Simcoe needed to lure his old comrades in the Queen's Rangers, the British military unit he led during the American Revolutionary War. His enticements were park-sized lots of land fronting Lot Street and stretching north to what would soon be Bloor Street, along with jobs. His old Rangers became new again, with a mandate to build roads using labour supplied by those good citizens of Toronto convicted of common assault or for being drunk in public. Toronto had a very small jail, and road gangs were found to be expedient for temporarily ridding the town of undesirables, of which there was never a shortage. Simcoe's Rangers built many roads, all of which the governor, in an unmilitary fashion, took great delight in naming after members of the English aristocracy, English government functionaries, himself, his wife and his friends, and there was even one for the town's brewmaster—Joseph Bloore.

In 1796, illness forced Governor Simcoe to return to England, and though Toronto continued to grow, it suffered from the absence of his military discipline and degenerated into a back-woods stinker. City roads were ill kept, creeks and streams were polluted by raw sewage, most water wells became contaminated by outdoor privies, and the lake water was poisoned by the disposal of dead animals and garbage on winter ice. During the second year of the War of 1812, the Americans landed a sizeable enough force to take the town, by then named York. They burned government buildings and looted military and private provisions, actions that many historians point to as the cause for the subsequent counterattack by British and militia troops on the U.S. capital of Washington. Tit for tat, but the sacking of York provided some benefit to residents because rebuilding efforts included fixing streets and covering sewer canals that fed into local streams and rivers. York, now called Toronto, still stunk of raw sewage, but residents no longer feared stepping in the filth except during periods of heavy rainfall.

However, the covered canal sewer system poured even more effluent into Lake Ontario, creating another problem. Raw sewage spreads cholera, and, in 1832, Irish immigrants brought the disease to Toronto's population of 5000 people, where it killed 20 residents a day until the winter of 1833–34. Survivors carried on as best they could, and that included chopping ice from a lake polluted with cholera-bearing raw sewage. In the spring of 1834, the cholera epidemic returned, killing so many residents that victims were buried in mass graves, the largest being the "Great Hole" next to St. James Cathedral on Church Street and the town's Potter's Field, then known as Strangers' Field, at a place now called Yorkville. During the 1870s, the bodies buried in Strangers' Field were dug up and moved to the Great Hole, a site that today contains the remains of over 6000 of Toronto's poor along with victims of the 1932–34 cholera disaster and the 1918 Spanish influenza epidemic.

On a brighter side, the 1832–34 cholera epidemic provided Toronto a valuable lesson in biology; residents stopped emptying privy and slop buckets into streets and canals, city fathers began to look at building a proper sewage system, and people stopped drinking local water, a boon for both brewers and farmers. Wealthy residents drank fresh water hauled in from the countryside, while the less affluent drank the product of Toronto's many large breweries, a fortuitous change for local farmers as it put them on the road to riches by supplying breweries with grain, especially barley. Area farmers grew other crops to facilitate Toronto's insatiable demand for alcoholic beverages, namely corn and rye to provide mash for legal and illegal distilleries, but barley was king. The fear of cholera drove Toronto's citizens to drink beer at home, at work and at the city's many taverns (one for every 50 residents). Taverns offered male residents warmth in winter, free bar food, a taste of old-country decor and the opportunity to socialize with their political and fraternal peers, be they

Tory conservatives, Whig reformers or members of fraternal organizations, the Freemasons and Orangemen. Entry to most Toronto taverns was barred to Reformers (Liberals) and Catholics, who confined their socialist activities to prohibitionist and church groups—a polarizing effect that saw taverns become the driving force behind Toronto's political system.

At its incorporation in 1834, Toronto, with a population of 9200, had 78 licensed taverns and probably an equal number of unlicensed establishments—one for every 60 residents. Each one catered to a distinct social class, with English and Scottish Protestants dominating. If a resident wanted to enter into the political system of Upper Canada, he began his quest in a Toronto "Protestants only" tavern. Tavern politics governed Toronto, and the city's incorporation laws awarded elected officials the powers of a European city-state. Toronto's elected mayor and alderman proclaimed bylaws, and as automatic magistrates, they enforced those laws, a system known as "the Family Compact." This system was a political force that evaded provincial control for decades but would later come under the influence of "secret societies," the Freemasons and the Loyal Order of Orangemen. By 1841, when the provincial government conducted an inquiry into Toronto's political system, there were 140 licensed taverns with probably an equal number of unlicensed establishments, one for every 25 residents over the age of 16 and all under the control of Toronto's alderman/magistrate-appointed police force, an organization controlled by the Orange Order.

The Orange Order came into its own with the massive Irish immigration into Toronto following the Irish potato blight of 1845. A Catholic and poor man's form of Freemasonry, the order became entrenched in Toronto constabulary and launched its own politicos from taverns into lower-level municipal politics. The Family Compact lost control of both taverns and the police, and chaos ruled Toronto as the Order attempted to control upper levels of government. Between 1836 and 1860, there were no fewer than 26 major riots in Toronto, almost all involving the Orange Order.

Closer to the 20th century, Toronto's political system became a monster with the head of a puppy (Protestant conservatives), the body of a crocodile (Protestant and Catholic reformists) and the tail of a dragon (the Catholic Orange Order). Bylaws passed by Conservatives saw immediate repeal by Reformists, while the Orange Order–controlled police force followed its own political agenda. To get anything done for the good of the city required the stern hand of the province, and in 1858, the Provincial Municipal Law was amended to allow for the formation of a police commission empowered to rein in Toronto's police force without prejudice from council members. That worked, and over the years, Toronto City Council would create more commissions to circumvent political infighting: water, public transit, harbour, gas and electric commissions. Commissions are a weird political adjunct born of tavern politics and used by Toronto City Council for nearly all of the 20th century.

Historically, if something needed doing in Toronto, it was delegated to a commission, and these delegations would eventually become the more than 40 boards or agencies controlled by one "king of the castle" commissioner—the city manager. Today, council members still tavern talk and bicker, but usually over money and taxes, while the day-to-day operation of the mega-city is left to City Manger Joe Pennachetti, a man for all seasons and the real King of Toronto.

What's in a Name?

I threw the opening pitch at a Blue Jays game, and after the pitch, the mascot asked me if I wanted him to sign the game ball, which I thought was funny. What would he write? "Best Wishes, Some Guy in a Bird Suit"?

–Ken Jennings, *Jeopardy!* champion

THE TORONTO NAME GAME

The earliest version of the name "Toronto" first appeared on a 1670 French map of the Great Lakes area as "Lac de Taranteau," indicating the entire geographical area of Lake Ontario and the Humber River north to Lac de Taranteau, now Lake Simcoe. French cartographers mapping unknown areas habitually copied down the place names used by indigenous peoples, and while that 1670 French cartographer undoubtedly visited the area, probably camping at the Iroquois village of Teiaiagon on the Humber River, he got his name information from a Mohawk Iroquois rather than a Seneca.

The First Nations village of Teiaiagon occupied the area of land where modern-day Bloor Street crosses the Humber River, an area later called Baby Point after the Honourable James Baby constructed a large home overlooking the river. First inhabited by Iroquois bands of Mohawk and Seneca, then later by a band of the Anishinabe Nation called the Mississauga, Teiaiagon was, at various times, a sizeable village with as many as 50 longhouses and a formidable palisade for protection.

Two Iroquois bands shared the village of Teiaiagon, and while the Seneca called the area Glyando, the Mohawks used the word Tkaronto, meaning "the fishing place you arrived at by paddling up the river," referring to the Humber River. The Humber was a well-travelled water route to Lac Taranteau on the way to Georgian Bay and was named by Governor Simcoe because it reminded him of England's river of that name. Years earlier, fur traders had erected a small fort at the mouth of the Humber that they called the Taranteau Passage. That name stuck until 1750, when the French constructed another larger fort west of the small fur-trading fort, garrisoned it with a dozen soldiers, brought in a few settler families to grow food and renamed it Fort Rouillé after the French colonial minister. The settlers did miserably because the clay soil yielded poor crops, but thanks to the fort's location at the mouth of the Humber, fur trading quickly accelerated, with 150 bales shipped out annually, a huge amount when compared to the 20 bales shipped from British-controlled Kingston. In 1758, when word reached Fort Rouillé's commander, a Captain Douville, that English forces were about to take Fort Niagara, he ordered his fort burned and hightailed it for Montréal. This action marked the end of the French era and the beginnings of a great city called…Toronto.

Little York

The name Little York was quickly adopted by residents after the 1793 name change from Toronto to York as a way to dissociate the town from the many other communities and counties with the same name.

Dirty Little York

The adjective "dirty" was added to the dissociative name and commonly used by 19th-century residents to signify their disgust with the town's open sewers, street-side garbage dumps and roads strewn with smelly horse buns.

Muddy York

The name Muddy York was commonly used by both residents and visitors to signify their unhappiness with the abysmal road conditions of a town built on the former lake bottom of old Lake Iroquois. Clay made for good roads in dry weather, but a little rain turned those same roads into a thick, wheel-stopping mix of clay and horse and ox manure that made crossing streets a nightmare for residents.

Little Amsterdam

In 1831, grain miller James Wort arrived from Britain with a pair of gigantic millstones and set up shop at the eastern end of Toronto's waterfront. To power his huge grindstones, he constructed a windmill, and unlike the common Dutch variety, his was such an immense structure that on clear days it was visible from the American side of Lake Ontario. Constructed of brick, 22 metres high and with four great sails, Wort's windmill was a triumph of engineering and so welcome a landmark to the city's dreary waterfront that residents began calling their town "Little Amsterdam." However, the gristmill needed such high winds to turn its sails that flour production was limited even after the installation of a steam engine in 1832. Sadly, the failure of his fantastic windmill caused James Wort to become despondent, and when his wife died in childbirth in 1832, he threw himself down a well at the mill.

Hogtown

At the time of Canadian Confederation in 1867, the population of Toronto, then called York, hovered around 45,000, with 98 percent being of British stock. One of those Brits, butcher and St. Lawrence Market stall owner William Davies, had a notion to make Toronto the pork-processing capital of Canada. By 1875, he had expanded his Don River slaughterhouse at 145 Front Street East, a well-constructed edifice that still casts a shadow over a street once so filled with swine that it earned Toronto the odious moniker. A few years later, half the pork products shipped to Britain came from the William Davies Company. In 1879, Davies constructed a new packing plant and invented peameal bacon, a Canadian original.

In 1921, the animals got their revenge on the millionaire meat-packer. While travelling by car in the southern U.S., the elderly Davies stopped to relieve himself at the roadside, turning his back on a large billy goat. The goat took advantage of the situation and butted Davies. Davies died of his injuries a few days later. Death by billy goat, a weird but somehow fitting end for William Davies, a historical luminary in a city he caused to be nicknamed "Hogtown."

The Big Smoke

During the latter part of the 19th century, immigration to Toronto soared and people arrived expecting green trees, clean waters and fresh air. Instead, they found an insanely busy harbour with soot-belching smokestacks, polluted water and air thick with coal and wood smoke. Immigrants from England's industrial cities and towns were so at home in Toronto they began using the same nickname they afforded England's largest industrial city, London, "the Big Smoke." That nickname hung on until 1904, when the Great Fire turned the Big Smoke name into reality.

Wild Streets

I don't want to go to Toronto
I don't want to go
All of the blocks are square
None of the streets are twisted
None of the streets are paved with bricks

–Radio Free Vestibule
"I Don't Want To Go To Toronto"

THE ROAD TO CIVILIZATION

Falling in Line

Toronto owes its neat, block-street structure to its founder Lieutenant-Governor, Colonel John Graves Simcoe. Ever the militarist, Governor Simcoe saw to it that Toronto's streets were equally spaced in a military fashion, with a grand promenade leading to what would eventually be the seat of government. To entice fellow officers to settle in his new town, he provided them with park-sized lots north of a straight line that he drew above his new village of York, a line he called Lot Street, a name later changed to Queen Street in honour of Queen Victoria's ascension to the throne of Britain.

The Way North

Today, while most of Toronto's almost 5700 kilometres of roads follow Governor Simcoe's standard grid pattern, there are weird exceptions, such as meandering Dundas Street and Davenport Road, both of which follow paths taken by generations of First Nations peoples. In the early days, the many rivers and streams emptying into Lake Ontario featured huge salmon runs, and First Nations bands would travel hundreds of kilometres to catch and dry the fish for the coming winter. Ancient, well-worn trails connected all the rivers from the St. Lawrence to Lake Erie, with many wide enough for a settler's wagon and ox team.

Those first settlers must have been ecstatic to find highways into the wilderness, but land grants along these easy routes went quickly, and, taking a page from the First Nations trail system, the government looked north to build new roads. They were called "colonization roads," and crews began swinging axes and laying corduroy over swampy sections in the spring of 1851. The City of Toronto had a vital interest in colonization roads as they provided a solution to the "Irish problem"—that is, what to do with the thousands of Irish refugees from the Great Famine. City council simply arranged provincial land grants and transportation for arriving immigrants and sent them north to a promised land of plenty. It would be an unmitigated disaster; Irish settlers could grow only subsistence crops on their scrubby northern farms, and within a few years, they were back to being such a problem that the subject of roads was almost verboten at city council meetings for decades.

From Rails to Roads

City council soon became transfixed by the railway's philosophy of "Who needs roads when you've got trains?" and though trolley cars were good, streets were considered old fashioned and a frivolous expense. That mindset continued until the 1893 Columbian Exposition in Chicago spawned the City Beautiful Movement that shamed U.S. cities into sprucing up their infrastructures, a movement that spread to Toronto and precipitated the formation of the Guild of Civic Arts, a group of artists and architects concerned about the dilapidated condition of their city. The guild acquired political clout by hiring Sir Aston Webb, an English architect famous for the redesign of London's Buckingham Palace. Webb put forward the idea of building a grand avenue from Front Street to Queen's Park to be called Federal Avenue and to include a civic centre, similar to New York's Times Square. He further proposed the reworking of parks, several street extensions and a few gardened carriage routes, or parkways, and the conversion of York Street into another grand avenue. He also suggested something novel for Toronto—roads cutting through street grids on a diagonal, called radial thoroughfare.

The city actually began working on plans for the great Federal Avenue with its imposing rendition of New York's Times Square, and later the plans for the York Street conversion, calling it Cambria Avenue. What might have made Toronto glorious actually existed on paper but got no further because of the city's financial problems. The city would eventually extend some roads, rework a few parks, construct some radial roads and build a gardened carriage way called Lakeshore Drive, but generally Toronto, and especially its roads, remained dilapidated because of city council's fixation on railways. The city was a railway town plain and simple, but then a whirlwind struck the city, and its name was the "stink wagon," the moniker given to the automobile, the great force that caused the Toronto to rethink its allegiance to the mighty railways and begin modernizing the city's streets.

STREETS OF NOTE

Dundas Street

Named for Henry Dundas, Viscount Melville, one of Governor
Simcoe's bosses back in England, Dundas is a road that defies
Toronto's normal grid street system by meandering like a snake,
beginning west of Ossington Avenue. Built to connect Newark
with Governor Simcoe's proposed capital of London and York,
the street terminated at the Humber River settlement of Lambton
Mills where it intersected with Lot Street. Nowadays, Dundas is
a major Yonge Street intersection crossed by 60 million pedestrians annually via scramble lights, but it never existed in the city
until the early 20th century when the City Beautiful Movement
caused Toronto to depart from tradition and construct some
unorthodox roadways. After the arrival of the automobile, Dundas
began to snake its way toward Yonge Street and the city centre
by the cobbling together of existing roadways, some up, some
down and a few with dramatic turns that combine to make driving Dundas a weird snakes-and-ladder experience in a city ruled
by a grid street system.

The Danforth

Danforth Avenue, once called the Danforth Road, is a legacy of Asa Danforth, an American scallywag from Syracuse, New York, who in 1779, somehow convinced Upper Canada's administrator Peter Russell that he was an able engineer and the right man for the job of constructing a road from York to Kingston. Asa and his men built a road, but it was just a muddy trail and so far from the lake as to be almost useless to settlers. The next year, with his professional engineering credentials in question, Asa skipped town, but he left behind his name for the company that actually constructed both the city connection of Danforth Avenue to the Kingston Road and the Kingston Road itself, the Don and Danforth Plank Road Company.

Davenport Road

Lake Ontario is a puddle remnant of a far greater body of water that historians call Lake Iroquois, a receding glacial meltwater lake that provided the earliest First Nations people a shoreline trail between the Don and Humber rivers. During Toronto's formative years, 1790 to 1830, the shoreline was a problem for settlers because along the harbour, the First Nations path ran atop an escarpment, which had a drop of 6 metres to the beach. When the path became Front Street, that drop to the beach required extensive grading, with the beach becoming the Esplanade.

West of Yonge Street, and originally called the "Plank Road" by settlers, the street was renamed Davenport Road after the name of the original house built around 1797 by Ensign John McGill, a member of Governor Simcoe's road-building Queen's Rangers. Ensign McGill named his home after either a Major Davenport of that same company, as many historians claim, or a local builder named Davenport who probably built his home.

Starting in the mid-19th century, improvements to Davenport Road were financed by road tolls collected at five gates along the way. Toll collectors, or gatekeepers, resided in nearby cottages, one of which still stands at the northwest corner of Bathurst Street and Davenport Road. From Davenport Road, affectionately called "the Dav" by locals, travellers have only to look north to see the Lake Iroquois escarpment, the onetime shore of a much deeper Lake Ontario.

During the 1890s, the area of the city where the Northern Railway and the CPR met at Davenport Road and Dufferin Street (the Junction) began attracting Italian immigrants to work on the railways. By 1913, the area's Italian population had swelled to over 10,000, and while half were permanent residents, the other half (mostly males, called "sojourners") returned to Italy every fall and made the trip back in early spring—Toronto's first commuters.

Yonge Street

In 1793, at his headquarters in the newly named town of York, Lieutenant-Governor John Graves Simcoe leaned over an area map and ran a finger along a vertical line marking a First Nations trail (the Indian Road) between York and Lake Simcoe. Then he turned to a subordinate, explained that it was their only way out of town should the Americans show up, and ordered it made into a proper road. When questioned by the subordinate as to how this was to be accomplished, Simcoe probably looked out the window, pointed at a newly arrived settler driving a wagon and ox team and said, "Simple really, we make them build it. Make the construction of 30 feet (9 metres) of my road a condition for a land grant. Oh, and call the road Yonge Street. Sir George will like that." Sir George Yonge, at the time Britain's Secretary of War and an expert on Roman roads, was probably flattered to have his name associated with such a significant undertaking. It was important for the time because ongoing conflict with the U.S. made a quick escape route out of town imperative, and it was also essential for Ontario's future because the road gave rise to the concession, or grid system, of provincial roadways.

Construction of Yonge Street began at another of Simcoe's lines on a map, a horizontal line denoting the northern town limits. He named this street Eglinton, and not after Scotland's famed castle as some historians supposed, but after Hugh Montgomerie, 12th Earl of Eglinton, a fellow officer of Simcoe's during the American Revolutionary War and later Lieutenant-Governor of Edinburgh Castle in Scotland's capital. Yonge Street construction began in earnest but soon petered out because of a lack of effort by settlers. As a remedy, Governor Simcoe drew another line at the forest edge and named it Lot Street, after the park-sized lots of land he would use to entice his old officer comrades from the war with the 13 colonies to relocate to York. They would come and oversee the road's construction, and for labour to clear bush, Simcoe would give them carte blanche to press-gang criminals and drunks. After the War of 1812, Yonge Street became the primary route north for North West Company fur traders, an issue that caused occasional food shortages in the city because the company hired farmers with wagons to haul their boats to Lake Huron.

Mostly complete by 1816, Yonge Street would eventually run on for 1896 kilometres, ending at Rainy River on the Ontario–Minnesota border, and for a century, it was billed as the world's longest street, a weird urban myth promulgated by the *Guinness Book of Records* until 1998. Yonge Street is a road that begins in Toronto and ends at Rainy River, and though it is long, it goes by other names past Barrie, and for that reason fails to qualify as the world's longest street.

Queen Street

Originally called Lot Street by the unimaginative Lieutenant-Governor John Graves Simcoe, the road served as the horizontal baseline for Toronto's grid street system. Lot Street soon became Burlington Street as the Governor's road-building Queen's Rangers pushed it west toward the settlement of Burlington, a small lakeside settlement east of Hamilton with an important military installation. In 1837, the road received a final name change to that of Queen Street to honour Queen Victoria's coronation.

In those early days, there was nothing weird about the street; wide and straight as an arrow, it fronted some of the city's finest homes, while across the street, the servants employed in those fine homes built their small cottages. The weirdness began in 1883 when Timothy Eaton, a successful Yonge Street dry goods merchant, bought the northeast corner at the intersection of Yonge and Queen Streets and constructed a retail marvel, a department store. In 1894, Timothy Eaton's main competitor, Robert Simpson, opened a similar department store operation on the southeast corner, an edifice designed by Toronto architect Edmund Burke using an innovative curtain-wall construction that allowed for many large windows. By 1911, the two stores, employing almost 20,000 people, served as a welcoming gate for Queen Street shoppers, inviting them to browse not just the department stores, but also the many retail establishments that supplanted the fine homes and servant cottages from Yonge Street to Spadina Road. Nowadays, almost the entire length of Queen Street is devoted to shopping, and while those welcoming department store gates are but a memory, the invitation to browse endures.

The Trail of Tears

In 1853, the Upper Canada legislature passed the Public Lands Act to provide free land grants to settlers along kilometres of newly constructed colonization roads. However, word had leaked down from road construction crews that northern Ontario was mostly swamp, rocky and useless for agriculture.

To allay the fears of those settlers arriving and departing from Toronto, the city government conceived a program of lies and innuendo handed out as pamphlets. The imaginative copy on those pamphlets included weird slogans designed to bolster the confidence of settlers: "Where pines grow any crop will flourish," "Snow is fertilizer" and my favourite, "Swamp sickness [malaria] is caused by bad air, so clearing trees will fix that problem."

The colonization program was an unmitigated disaster, and while some settlers managed to eke out an existence growing vegetables for lumber crews, by 1890 the crews had cut all the white and red pine and moved south to Toronto to work in either William Davis' abattoir or the Gooderham and Worts distillery. Most of the hapless colonization-road settlers abandoned their farms and followed the lumber crews south to the big city.

Toronto's first sidewalk ran along the west side of Yonge from King to Queen Street and was made of tree bark. This strange and slippery walkway, an 1834 incorporation gift to the city by leather tanner and local philanthropist Jesse Ketchum, was made of his surplus hemlock tanning bark. *Good idea,* thought city council, and immediately hired David Gibson, the Provincial Land Surveyor, to design and build more sidewalks using less-slippery wood planks.

Main Street Redress

Almost every community in Britain and North America has a roadway named High Street or Main Street that bisects its business section. Toronto has a Main Street with a subway stop, but it is so far in the city's east end that it hardly qualifies as a main or high street. So as not to be found wanting by Ontario's municipal mainstream, Toronto's city councillors voted in 2002 to change the name of the section of Yonge Street between Crescent Road and Woodlawn Avenue to that of Rosedale Main Street.

NAMESAKES

Bloor Street

Bloor Street, originally a toll road running from Joseph Bloore's brewery to his land development project at Yorkville, had several names: the unimaginative Tollgate Road; St. Paul's Road, after St. Paul's Anglican Church; Sydenham Street, after Lord Sydenham, Governor of Canada; and finally around 1855, Bloore Street, after Joseph Bloore. Shortly thereafter, the "e" disappeared from the street name, probably because of a cartographer's error.

Bulwer Street

Bulwer Street, at Queen and Spadina, is named for Edward Bulwer-Lytton, English poet, playwright, novelist and, in 1858, the Secretary of England's colonies. Bulwer-Lytton is best remembered for penning the worst ever opening line of a novel, "It was a dark and stormy night…"

Christie Street

Yes, Mister Christie makes good cookies, and starting in 1849, he baked them for the entire country and fully deserves his memorial street at Bathurst and Bloor for the smiles he put on the faces of Canadian children.

Front Street

Front Street, originally christened as such by the unimaginative Governor Simcoe because it fronted his new lakeside outpost of York, changed names as it progressed eastward: King Street to honour King George III, and later Palace Street, because it led to the Parliament Buildings at the foot of Berkeley Street. Nowadays, it is all Front Street—a misnomer because the roadway no longer fronts the city.

Little Norway Crescent

Little Norway Crescent at Bathurst and Lake Shore Boulevard is named for the Norwegian Air Force training grounds established there during World War II. By 1941, when the facility moved to Gravenhurst, over 1000 Norwegian pilots were training at the Island Airport.

Longboat Avenue

Longboat Avenue at Parliament and Front Streets is named after First Nations runner Thomas Charles Longboat who won the Boston Marathon in 1907.

Mount Pleasant Road

Mount Pleasant Road between Bayview and Yonge is named for the 80-hectare Mount Pleasant Cemetery the road cut through in 1916. Designed by famous cemetery and garden architect Henry Englehart, the cemetery is Toronto's answer to New York's Central Park, but with lots of granite to keep it cool in summer. Among its almost 170,000 unseen inhabitants are many of the city's rich or famous, and looking for them among all the greenery has become an idyllic venture.

O'Hara Avenue

O'Hara Avenue at Queen and Lansdowne is named after Walter O'Hara, a serving officer with the Duke of Wellington in the Napoleonic Wars. He immigrated to Toronto in 1826, and by 1840, he had acquired 210 hectares north of Queen and west of Dufferin Street to subdivide into lots for home building. O'Hara named many area streets after the battles in which he fought, including Roncesville, Sorauren and Alhambra Avenues.

Pears Avenue

Pears Avenue at Davenport and Avenue Road is named for the Pears brothers, who operated a brickyard at that spot until the clay ran out and the company moved to Eglinton Avenue West. At the new Eglington location, the brothers produced 3 million red and yellow bricks per annum until the city purchased the property in 1926 to create Eglinton Park.

Pellatt Avenue

Pellatt Avenue at Albion and Weston Roads is named for Sir Henry Mill Pellatt, the man who brought electricity to Toronto and constructed the city's greatest monument to wild eccentricity, Casa Loma—his home from 1913 to 1923.

Price Street

Price Street at Summerhill Avenue and Yonge Street is named for Captain Joseph Price, who helped suppress the Rebellion of 1837 and owned the land from Summerhill to the Don River. After Price passed away, most of his land was subdivided into Chestnut Park, but his daughter held onto 4 hectares on Yonge Street and occupied a cottage on the spot where the North Toronto Railway Station stands, now reincarnated as the Summerhill LCBO outlet.

Richmond Street

Richmond Street, between King and Queen Streets, is named for Charles Lennox, the 4th Duke of Richmond and Governor-in-Chief of British North America in 1818. Lennox's tenure was short lived because the following year, while he was touring military installations, a soldier's pet fox bit him on the arm and he contracted rabies and died.

Rosedale

Rosedale Valley Road and was named by Mary Jarvis, wife of city luminary William Jarvis, for the many wild rose bushes covering the banks of the ravine that ran beside their home.

St. Clair Avenue

St. Clair Avenue received its name from a sign tacked onto a tree by young Albert Grainger, son of a local farmer, to denote his self-adoption of a middle name, that of the hero character

St. Clare in Harriet Beecher's then-popular novel *Uncle Tom's Cabin*. Only he got the spelling wrong, and in 1873, when surveyors came along to mark out Toronto's second concession road north of Bloor Street, they took Grainger's sign to be what locals called the existing trail and named the road St. Clair. In 1913, parishioners with either a sense of humour or a penchant for correct spelling erected St. Clare's Catholic Church, at 1118 St. Clair Avenue West.

St. George Street

St. George Street is named for Laurent Quetton St. George, a French loyalist who escaped from France to England, where he received a land grant along the St. Lawrence River. St. George engaged in the fur trade and did so well that he moved to York and set up shop as a merchant, opening several branch stores and constructing the city's first brick building, in 1818, at King and Fredrick Streets, from bricks he imported from the U.S.

STREET SMART

The Long and Short of It

Toronto's present-day road infrastructure is 5365 kilometres in length with 10,033 streets, the longest being Lawrence Avenue East (25 kilometres) and the shortest, Sea Grassway (9.72 metres). Sea Grassway is in the Jane and Finch area, an eyeblink off Dune Grassway.

Gates to Nowhere

The imposing gates on the north side of Queen Street West at the head of Strachan Avenue (pronounced *strawn*) at Trinity-Bellwood Park are the only remains of Trinity College, a Buckingham Palace lookalike building torn down in the 1950s.

Pass the Bugs

During the 1880s, the city installed dozens of new cast iron horse troughs along major streets. Each one included a drinking-fountain tap and a metal cup attached by a sturdy chain. The drinking tap and cup idea came from the city's medical health officer Dr. William Caniff, who thought easily available clean water would curtail disease.

A Good Idea

Until 1903, all of Toronto's streets were paved with brick, cedar blocks or the standard macadam crushed stone. In 1903, the city contracted with the newly formed Barber Asphalt Paving Company for the asphalt paving of 26 kilometres of municipal roadways.

Horse Buns to Ritzy

The Bridle Path, once a trail in the boondocks for horseback riding, became the city's ritziest address after E.P. Taylor constructed his lavish Windfields Estate there in 1936. Torontonians and tourists wanting a peek at this enclave of exclusivity must enter off Post Road, or Lawrence Avenue East, near Edwards Gardens.

Ploughs and Stars

Massey Street at King and Strachan is the spot that family patriarch Daniel Massey chose to construct his farm-machinery company. His son, Hart Almerrin Massey, grew the company into Canada's largest manufacturer of farm implements, and, in 1891, he merged the company with its chief competitor to form Massey-Harris, the world's largest corporation of its kind. The Massey family is best known to Torontonians through Hart's grandsons, Vincent Massey, Canada's first homegrown Governor General, and Raymond Massey, the famous Hollywood actor.

Like a Phoenix

Spadina Avenue, nowadays running from Queen's Quay to Eglinton Avenue, originally ran from Bloor Street to the top of the escarpment. It was constructed in 1836 by Doctor William Baldwin to reach his new home called Spadina, a First Nations word meaning "hill" that is actually pronounced *spadeena*. Baldwin's home burned in 1835 and was rebuilt and given to his son Robert, who passed away in 1858, with the property then sold to James Austin, the president of the Dominion Bank. Austin completely reconstructed Spadina House into the grand mansion that today sits just east of Casa Loma.

The Fork in the Road

York Street, at King Street and University Avenue, was originally the turnoff from Lot Street that travellers took to reach York, while those heading east to Kingston stayed on the straight and narrow.

Ooh-la-la

University Avenue, running north from Front Street to College Street, was constructed in 1829 as a grand French-style drive above Queen Street leading to the Queen's University campus and, in 1886, to the Ontario Legislative Building, better known as Queen's Park.

Lost 'Hoods

The only reason Toronto is no longer the dullest city on Earth is that it is no longer full of Anglo-Canadians. It is full of Hong Kong Chinese. And not a few Italians.

–Joel Garreau, journalist

ANNEXATION ANARCHY

For all of the 19th century and most of the 20th, Toronto was the centre of a spider web of roads connecting a bevy of small towns and villages. As many as 50 villages circled the prime community of York; they are now called neighbourhoods or have been completely forgotten but for quaint notations on street signs.

Town and Country

During the city's formative years, its incoming population was polarized by income; residents with money, either from family or the military, headed into the core and constructed as close to old country homes as they could afford, while those who were less well endowed gravitated into the countryside to work the land. Settlements abounded on the periphery; areas with moving water to power a mill needed a road, and roads attracted settlers. Like its core counterpart, rural society emulated the Old Country by constructing English-style churches, homes, mills and taverns.

When cholera ravaged the core of the city in the 1830s, many downtown residents headed for the countryside to buy up land grants and establish country home estates close to the city. This new rural gentry required labour to work expanded fields, and this attracted newly arrived immigrants, swelling the populations of quaint villages until they became incorporated towns with a post office and a municipal government. Of those towns, seven were destined to become representative parts of Metropolitan Toronto: Leaside, Weston, Mimico, New Toronto, Forest Hill, Swansea and Long Branch.

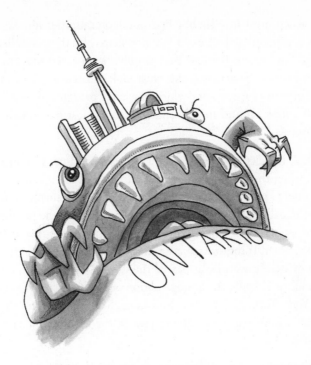

Urban Creep

Many villages and towns were just too distant to interest the growing city, and hung on until the latter part of the 19th century, when the core became industrialized and began to creep into the countryside searching for labour and an increased tax base. Out from the core went new streets, bridges, railways and sheriffs with annexation orders. From 1891 to 1921, there were 22 annexations to the city, doubling its size from 50 to 100 square kilometres. The urbanites called it progress, a view not shared by most residents of those quaint towns because the city offered them few services. Many tried to fight annexation, but the all-powerful City of Toronto was legally empowered by the province to gobble up smaller communities like so many cookies.

Although some larger outlying settlements did survive into the 21st century to become places of interest, 21st-century progress has turned most into shabby bedroom communities for the city's overpopulated core—a fate not shared by those smaller villages and towns because they simply disappeared into the fog of history. Nowadays, one must look at street signs to identify Toronto's former rural glory, but once recognized, it is worth a look around to appreciate what was lost in the name of progress.

In 1922, the city stopped annexing villages and towns—until 1953, when the provincial government passed a bill creating a two-tiered government for the six municipalities surrounding Toronto, calling it Metropolitan Toronto. In 1992, the province passed legislation requiring Metro to take in a larger area, calling it the Greater Toronto Area, also known as the GTA. In 1997, the provincial government passed the City of Toronto Act, and on January 1, 1998, the amalgamation of the municipalities of East York, York, North York, Etobicoke, Scarborough and the regional municipality of Toronto created the new City of Toronto in the GTA.

Politically, the GTA is currently represented by 45 Members of Parliament, 44 Members of Provincial Parliament and five senators, while the GTA's constituent municipalities, including Toronto, have their own mayors and city councils. On the weird side, while Toronto has become one huge mega-city—the GTA, the fifth largest city in North America—old municipal addresses are still required by both Canada Post and utility companies.

STILL HANGING ON

Yorkville

Today, Yorkville is a trendy downtown shopping area, but in 1810, it was a tollgate at the crossroads of Indian Road (Yonge Street) and Second Concession Road (Bloor Street)—a watering hole called the Red Lion Inn where thirsty travellers could rest and a cemetery for those unfortunates who were unable to afford a church burial. At that time, York residents were either rich or poor, and with the general population mostly strapped for cash, the cemetery was simply the "General Plot" or "General Burying Grounds" to city cartographers. York had plenty of bodies, and digging holes required labourers, who in turn required a place to live.

Old Yorkville was every kid's nightmare, a community of ghouls, things that go bump in the night and the subject of many ghost stories. Settlers avoided the place, and while land values shot up all around, Yorkville land remained a bargain, which attracted the attention of Joseph Bloore, a local brewer, and William Jarvis, the local sheriff and a sometime land speculator. The pair bought the entire area for a song, put in a proper street, subdivided for building lots and began selling.

However, lot sales were slow, and around 1840, the developers decided that Yorkville needed some industry. They provided cheap land for a brickyard that attracted labourers in spite of the spooky stories. The influx of workers helped, but what the area really needed was to get rid of the cemetery, an inevitability that the pair began to advertise and people bought, expecting its removal. In reality, the cemetery was not removed until the 1870s when residents stopped drinking water from corpse-tainted wells and the province ordered the cemetery closed and the bodies removed. A few thousand graves were exhumed and the remains taken away, but how many still RIP there is anyone's guess—perhaps as many as 5000, as they keep turning up at every modern-day Yorkville construction project. Born of the dead, and now shopped by Toronto's affluent, Yorkville has become a popular venue for the city's "ghost tour" companies.

O'Sullivan's Corners

A bustling little village at the crossroads of Sheppard Avenue and Victoria Park, O'Sullivan's Corners was established by Irish immigrant Patrick O'Sullivan, who constructed a hotel with a post office in 1892. Closed in 1912, the post office reopened in 1956 to service the first of the area's massive subdivision projects called Town and Country and Wishing Well Acres.

Famous 1920s midnight whisky purveyor Harry C. Hatch, owner of Toronto's Gooderham & Worts Distillery, owned a horse-breeding farm in this area that during the 1960s became another subdivision called Bridlewood Acres, from whence came a favourite son, the comedian and actor Mike Myers. O'Sullivan's Corners shares an unimaginative heritage designation with the Tam O'Shanter Golf Club and is now called Tam O'Shanter-Sullivan.

Thistletown

Originally called Coonats Corners after the original settler family and located at the junction of Albion Road and Islington Avenue in North Etobicoke Township, Thistletown was erased during the rush to modernization in the 1950s. The old town was sacrificed in the name of progress by a force known as Rexdale, property developer Rex Heslop's industrial sprawl that necessitated the widening of Albion Road and the destruction of Thistletown.

Vestiges of the old community are still around, hiding on side roads or tucked behind hedges; one must simply look hard to find them. One such remnant, and not at all difficult to find, is the house at 23 Jason Road, circa 1802, Thistletown's first residence and one of Toronto's oldest homes. One only has to look there to visualize Albion Road before its 1950s destruction by Rex Heslop—a man who did so much neighbourhood removal that his coined word "Rexdale" has become iconic to the entire area.

GONE BUT NOT FORGOTTEN

Armadale

Established in 1805 in what is now southeast Markham and was originally named Magdala until forced to make a postal name change, this village hosted many United Empire Loyalist settlers and became a prosperous community. Part of the suburban sprawl of modern Markham, most of Armadale has been destroyed, leaving only its historic church as a memorial.

Brockton Village

Incorporated as a town in 1881, Brockton had its roots in a Lot Street property awarded to James Brock, a member of Governor Simcoe's road-building Queen's Rangers and a cousin of Sir Isaac Brock, the hero of Queenston Heights. After James Brock's demise, his widow, Lucy, paid for the construction of Brock Avenue and began selling residential parcels, creating a small settlement she dubbed Brockton.

By the time it was incorporated as a town, Brockton had grown to a fair size, bordering High Park on the west, Dufferin to the east, Bloor to the north and Queen to the south. *Too big*, thought Toronto's city fathers, and three years after its incorporation, they annexed Brockton.

Gone but not forgotten, Brockton Village is remembered through street signage and the historical preservation of its town hall, located on the southwest corner of Brock Avenue and Bloor Street. Once the site of the great Dufferin Racetrack, the area is now home to the Dufferin Mall shopping complex.

Clairville

Established in 1850 at Albion Road (originally named Clairville Road) and Steeles Avenue, this unincorporated village was situated on a private estate owned by Jean du Petit Pont de la Haye, a teacher at Upper Canada College, and named after his daughter Clair. It featured a mill, several taverns, farms and a toll road west to Albion Township, now amalgamated into the Town of Caledon.

During the 1970s, the Humber River was dammed to create the village's legacy, the Clairville Reservoir, an action that drowned all traces of downtown Clairville. The house- and farm-studded eastern section of Clairville became an industrial area, and the western section is now the Clairville Conservation Area and the City of Brampton's housing sprawl.

Agincourt

This village began as an unnamed post office burg in the Sheppard–Markham Road area established by John Hill in 1858. When an imperious French-speaking Lower Canada postal official from Montréal demanded that his post office have a French name, Hill chose Agincourt, the name of the battlefield where the English soundly whipped the French. Although that irony was overlooked by postal officials, it served to make a local hero of postmaster Hill.

John Hill was a lucky man because he owned what two railway companies would soon come calling for—land on which to build their tracks. Hill got rich, and his little village received two railway stations that proved irresistible to produce-growing settlers. One of those stations would survive the years to become the Agincourt Station on the Stouffville GO Transit Line.

Dayton

Established in 1790 on the banks of the Humber River, Dayton had a narrow cart path into the city named Finch's Road after hotelier John Finch, who constructed a small hotel at the place where the trail met Yonge Street. The trail to Dayton would later become a concession road renamed Finch Avenue, and the village of Dayton would see a name change to Emery to avoid postal confusion with Dayton, Ohio.

In the early 1950s, Emery was removed by Highway 401 and zoning changes, and today it is a blighted industrial area with no existing remnant of the old town.

Malvern

Officially established in 1856, Malvern was already an important agricultural centre when general store owner David Brown opened a post office in his store. The next year sensing a financial opportunity, the reeve of Markham, David Reesor, later to be Senator Reesor, bought up all the surrounding land and began selling off lots to farmers while assuring them the railway would soon arrive to cement their prosperity. The railway never came, but the community still became an important food supplier for Toronto until the 1950s, when the Canada Mortgage and Housing Corporation expropriated all the area farms to build a model subdivision.

Bedford Park

A small village at the junction of Yonge Street and Lawrence Avenue became Bedford Park after brothers Phillip and Mathew Ellis constructed a hotel and tavern in 1873 that they called the Bedford Park Hotel. Partners in Birks-Ellis-Ryrie, a retail jewellery company that would eventually become Birks Jewellers, the brothers bought all the land north of Lawrence to Woburn between Yonge and Bathurst Streets with an eye to developing a factory town with hundreds of small homes for workers.

However, in 1890, Bedford Park, along with the villages of Davisville and Eglington, were amalgamated as North York, and the new town council vetoed the Ellis brother's factory idea but allowed them to proceed with their plan to build the hundreds of small homes. Today, the Ellis brothers' memorial street, Bedford Park Avenue, runs between Yonge Street and Avenue Road, with most of their small bungalows no replaced by much larger, so-called "monster" homes.

John Barleycorn

My brother and I used to say that drownin' in beer was like heaven, eh? Now he's not here, and I've got two soakers... this isn't heaven, this sucks.

–Bob MacKenzie, *The Adventures of Bob & Doug McKenzie: Strange Brew*

BIG BEER

Eighteenth-century settler farmers led a hard life in southern Ontario; although crops grew well, harvesting in quantities large enough to provide economic benefit proved difficult. Ontario farmers learned to be self-sufficient. They built cellars in which to store root vegetables and had plenty of children to forage for berries. Their wives knew how to cook game and bake good bread. To make flour for that bread, they needed what the government in Britain provided, the gristmills.

These mills served a dual purpose—they supplied the breweries to keep troops in beer rations and ground grain for the settlers, the former by contract, and the latter by tithe. Millers kept 10 percent of the farmer's grain in exchange for the grinding or grist—a good system that provided millers extra income through the sale of flour. However, with more settlers arriving daily, the tithe became a backlog subject to rot, so grist millers turned to distilling tithed grain using homemade stills. It was foul-tasting stuff, but area farmers had plenty of children to pick berries for the miller, and a little juice made the unpleasant brew somewhat palatable.

Miller's hooch soon flowed through the countryside and into communities until it finally reached Toronto, a filthy town already afloat in beer and rum, and rife with pollution. Raw sewage inundated almost every source of water in Toronto, so people turned to beer as an alternative. But the taxman took too big a bite from beer, and cheap, bootlegged whisky from the countryside was welcomed like an old friend.

Good for Your Health

Toronto was originally a French outpost with inhabitants obtaining drinking water from the Humber River or the Lake Ontario; and while the French enjoyed the odd bit of wine and brandy hauled down from Fort Frontenac, present-day Kingston, they were not big imbibers. All that changed when the English military moved in, a force with international experience on the physiological effects of drinking local water. Drinking local water made soldiers sick, while drinking beer kept them healthy, and that medical mindset resulted in a daily 2-litre beer ration for the troops. Where the British military went, their brewmasters followed, and in Canada the military moved west to Toronto, a geographical area that proved to be ideal for growing grain to make beer.

The Military Mindset

During Toronto's formative years, military brewmasters did double duty, brewing beer for both soldiers and settlers. As time progressed and settlers increased in numbers, brewmasters servicing the military quit to open taverns with small breweries located in back sheds or, like brewmasters Joseph Bloore, John Severn and Enoch Turner, to open stand-alone breweries. It was an equitable arrangement, as settlers eschewed the military mindset not to drink local water and confined their beer drinking to taverns. Toronto had enough beer, even for the Irish immigrants who began arriving by the shipload.

In 1832, Irish newcomers brought with them the dreaded cholera, which spread through the open sewers into community water sources. The military mindset of drinking beer to survive suddenly became that of Toronto's citizens, and tavern breweries were unable to keep up with demand. "Brew more" was the opportunistic shout heard loud and clear by every Toronto businessman, and big breweries popped up like mushrooms.

By the mid-19th century, 118 breweries were up and running in Canada West, with about 40 located in or around Toronto. Some, such as the Copeland and William Street breweries, were able to turn out 500 barrels per week. Toronto's new breweries put out a good product, made according to German purity laws by European-trained brewmasters using traditional methods, and it had an average alcohol content of nine percent.

The Consequences of Cholera

After the second cholera epidemic of 1834, Toronto's citizenry took to beer like fish to water with escalating demand polarizing city politics into imbibers and non-imbibers, Conservatives and Reformers.

In 1832, Yorkville blacksmith John Severn bought John Baxter's Rosedale brewery, and within several decades was turning out 500 barrels per week. In 1847, John Copeland built his new East End Brewery at King and Parliament Streets and began producing so many barrels that his operation would eventually need two hectares of underground storage.

In 1849, the city suffered another cholera outbreak followed by epidemics of typhus, diphtheria and smallpox. By 1860, almost the entire population had given up water for beer, and, in 1862, local businessman Eugene O'Keefe bought the Victoria Brewery, a small operation producing 1000 barrels annually. Within a year, he was producing over 7000 barrels of mostly lager beer annually. Eugene O'Keefe and his master brewers would go on upping beer production until 1911, the year O'Keefe constructed his new masterpiece brewery capable of producing half a million barrels annually.

BIG WHISKY

From Grain to the Gravy Train

In the 19th century, Toronto was awash in rotgut miller's whisky that sold for pennies a gallon almost anywhere, but then came a change for the better. In 1837, while experiencing an overstock of grain from bumper crops, flour millers William Gooderham and his brother-in-law partner, James Wort, son of the fantastic windmill builder James Wort Sr., decided to try their hand at distilling the good stuff. The Gooderham and Wort (G&W) partnership made very good stuff indeed, and while customers still had to pay the taxman, the vast quantities the partners produced allowed for low prices that turned G&W whisky into an international sensation. In 1861, the partners built a new distillery, the largest in Canada with its own wharf on Toronto Bay and a grain silo with a holding capacity of 80,000 bushels.

Bargain-priced, quality whisky made William Gooderham a rich man, but it turned his son and grandson, both named George William, into whisky kings and the richest men in Canada for decades. In its heyday, the company shipped out an excess of two million gallons annually to all points of the compass. G&W's massive whisky production would provide Ontario farmers with a rapid road to prosperity through the growing of various grains needed to distill spirits, the most important being rye and malting barley.

Wartime Woes

Beginning in 1914, G&W ran into hard times; the Great War in Europe had begun, and the distillery had to change production from whisky to acetone for the manufacture of explosives. At the war's end, the company returned to whisky production but encountered another setback when a 1920 Ontario liquor prohibition temporarily caused a complete halt to G&W's whisky production. Financially debilitating, these factors helped pave the way for the distillery to acquire a new owner.

Hatch-ing a Plan

In 1921, as prohibition got rolling in the U.S., a small whisky distillery in Bellville—Corby Distilleries Limited—sensed an opportunity and hired a successful rural liquor salesman named Harry C. Hatch as sales manager. An ambitious man, Hatch had almost single-handedly turned Ontario pharmacies into liquor dispensaries. A clause in Ontario's Prohibition Act allowed physicians to prescribe whisky for medicinal purposes, and thanks to Hatch, almost every Ontario doctor was writing prescriptions to be filled by pharmacists who supplied ice, mix and a nice place to imbibe, called a "soda fountain."

Harry Hatch soon had a river of Corby's whisky flowing south into the U.S., with a minor stream flowing into his pocket. He prospered because of prohibition and was soon able to buy

G&W for the tidy sum of $1.5 million. All good for Hatch, and a few years later, he bought the Hiram Walker Distillery in Walkerville. In 1927, he merged the two companies into Hiram Walker-Gooderham and Worts Limited to really capitalize on U.S. prohibition. America's national abstinence became a road to riches for Canadian whisky distillers, especially those owned by Harry C. Hatch, Joe Seagram's son, Edward, and the furniture-building Bronfman brothers of Montréal. The business triad shrunk to a more manageable scale in 1928 when the Bronfmans got the nod from their main U.S. distributor, Chicago mobster Al Capone, and bought Joseph E. Seagram & Sons.

In 1946, Harry Hatch died, but his whisky business carried on, and in 1957, with the bulk of operations shifted to Walkerville, G&W's Toronto operation stopped producing whisky and switched to distilling and bottling rum. In 1986, the giant English food conglomerate Allied-Lyons bought Hiram Walker-Gooderham and Worts, and a few years later, G&W stopped production altogether, with the Toronto facility beginning life anew as a film location. In 2001, the distillery complex, the finest surviving example of Victorian factory architecture in Canada, was acquired by property developers and refurbished into a top-flight Toronto tourist destination dubbed the Distillery District.

TAVERN TALES

City Icons

Of the hundreds of taverns that dotted Toronto streets in the early 19th century, only two have survived into modern times, the venerable Wheat Sheaf Tavern at King and Bathurst Streets and the nearby Black Bull Tavern at 298 Queen Street West, with both in continuous operation since the 1840s.

An early 19th-century stagecoach trip up Yonge Street north of Yorkville would have passengers begging for a tavern stop before the coach reached the infamous "hellhole." While passengers braced themselves with whisky for the coming ordeal, the driver would be outside tying tree branches to the wheels of the coach to prevent it from slipping off the steep, muddy road to the bottom.

If the descent went well, relieved passengers could stagger into another tavern at the bottom to prepare for the equally terrifying climb up the other side. In 1824, Scotsman James Hogg constructed a gristmill and whisky distillery at the bottom of the hellhole, and, in 1856, his two sons subdivided the property and sold off lots in what they called "Hogg's Hollow." There has been a tavern at the bottom of Hogg's Hollow since before the American invasion of 1813.

Deep-breath Drinking

In mid-19th-century city taverns, whisky sold for a penny a glass or five cents a grunt—a grunt being the amount of whisky a patron could drink in one breath.

No Drunks Allowed

During the early 19th century, city tavern owners found guilty of running disorderly houses were either fined or placed in the market square stocks on market day. While so indisposed, a tavern owner might be witness to the flogging of his customers for disorderly conduct.

DID YOU KNOW?

In 1951, Labatt Breweries, owner of the Winnipeg Blue Bombers football club, introduced Labatt Pilsner in a tall bottle with a blue label that soon garnered the nickname "Blue." That nickname stuck and became an iconic brand name, a fortuitous move for Labatt as it pointed the way for more sports they could colour blue. In 1977, Labatt Breweries kicked in money to help secure an American League baseball franchise for Toronto, while a "Name the Team" contest helped in selecting the name—Toronto "Blue" Jays.

Toronto Underground

Take a look at Yonge St., it looks like a flea market.
It's the longest street in the world, but it looks like hell.
There's a big store that hangs jeans and ladies' clothes
outside, and that's bullshit.

—former mayor Mel Lastman

LOST STREAMS

From Stream to Sewer

York was, for a time, blessed with a multitude of creeks, streams and rivers that provided early residents a seemingly endless supply of clean drinking water and succulent fish dinners. While the two largest waterways, the Don and Humber Rivers, were the original east-west boundaries of Toronto, dozens of smaller creeks ran in between. These creeks fed into streams that flowed to Lake Ontario, with almost all serving as ports for the multitude of small sailing craft that ferried goods to and from Kingston.

Alas, these creeks also proved convenient for the disposal of mill chaff, sawdust, sewage and abattoir effluent. By the middle of the 18th century, most of Toronto's streams and creeks had become open sewers that required covering over—an undertaking first acted upon after the cholera epidemics of the 1830s.

In 1838, the city constructed its first sewer, along King Street, and in 1840, a brick-lined drain was built along George Street that bisects the University of Toronto. Initially a timid undertaking thanks to costs, the city went at sewer installation vigorously after 1858, when Toronto brick maker Thomas Nightingale began manufacturing cheap clay sewer pipe. Unfortunately, costs dictated the combining of storm and waste sewers, with most of Toronto's once clean and bountiful creeks and streams buried and pressed into service as storm sewers.

Today, many of those streams and creeks are still functioning watercourses, with most completely entombed and running under the city in a great spider web of drains that a few curious explorers find irresistible. Although most of the underground streams can be entered through inspection manholes located along ravines and are spacious enough to walk in, it is not an advisable venture thanks to noxious odours, slippery footing and very large rats.

Garrison Creek

Garrison Creek rises north of St. Clair Avenue and runs for 7.7 kilometres, gathering water volume and sewage from various tributary openings and flowing under Christy Pits, Bickford, Fred Hamilton and Trinity Bellwoods parks before entering Toronto Harbour at the site of Old Fort York, also known as Stanley Barracks, from whence comes the name Garrison Creek (referring to soldiers).

Once a lush watercourse famed for its excellent fishing, Garrison Creek prompted Bishop John Strachan to build Trinity College on its west bank for the benefit of contemplative students. Unfortunately, those students did much of their contemplating on newly installed indoor plumbing that emptied into their contemplative stream, turning its once-pristine waters into an open sewer. Farther upstream, the breweries attracted by that same sparkling-clean water gave way to abattoirs and industry requiring a convenient waste disposal system, and, by 1880, the entire length of Garrison Creek had become a smelly sewer with its deep ravines proving irresistible for the disposal of foundation fill. At Christy Pits, a sand quarry with bridges over the creek, the city encased the stream in sewer pipe and buried both the creek and at least two of the stone bridges.

Today, the route of Garrison Creek is well marked by city Discovery Walk signage, and an ear to the ground almost anywhere will provide listeners an idea as to water volume. A good place to begin a tour is at Christy Pits Park, especially after a winter snowfall when warm creek water melts the snow, allowing the stream, a shadow of its former glory, to shout, "I'm still here! Help me!"

In 1954, when Hurricane Hazel inundated the city with torrential rain, Garrison Creek had a kind of temporary reprieve when water pressure blew manhole covers off the conduit, temporarily releasing the creek from bondage.

Taddle Creek

This watercourse rises from the old Lake Iroquois shoreline, or escarpment, above Davenport Road west of Bathurst Street, pools at Wychwood Park and then disappears into a 7-kilometre-long underground tunnel that runs parallel to Garrison Creek and into Lake Ontario. Once clean and lush, it enticed the University of Toronto to situate buildings along its ravine and to dam a section, called McCaul's Pond after the university's first president, to provide students an area for contemplative pause.

Then along came indoor toilets, and Taddle Creek became a drain of convenience with both the creek and McCaul's contemplative pond requiring a burial because of the stench. However, the creek would get its revenge during the 1920s, when its buried watercourse contributed to the cancellation of the T. Eaton Company's Art Deco–inspired skyscraper slated to rise above Eaton's College Street store.

Castle Frank Brook

Also known as Brewery or Severn Creek, Castle Frank Brook is sourced from three small streams and arises in the Dufferin-Lawrence area, flowing 12 kilometres through the Cedarvale Ravine and under the Nordheimer and Rosedale ravines before entering the Don River south of the Prince Edward Viaduct.

In 1830, Joseph Bloore built a red-brick brewery in the valley that Mary Jarvis—wife of the area's first resident and Sheriff of York, William Jarvis—named Rosedale after the profusion of wild roses found growing in the ravine, and while the brewery was in operation, the stream was called Brewery Creek.

Bloore sold his brewery in 1843 and joined with Sheriff William Jarvis to develop a nearby area they called Yorkville. When another, much larger brewery was constructed on the creek at Davenport Road, the stream took on the name Severn, after John Severn, the owner of that larger brewery.

DID YOU KNOW?

Rosehill Park, at Rosehill and St. Clair Avenues, is actually the 200-million-litre Rosehill Reservoir covered by a concrete cap in 1965 and layered over with soil and turf. Passersby lucky enough to find the city waterworks department conducting their periodic inspections are urged to ask for a peek inside.

STREAMS OF SHAME

Taylor Massey Creek

Called Silver Creek or Scarborough Creek in earlier times and renamed for the two large family estates through which it flowed, Taylor Massey Creek had its headwaters diverted into Highland Creek to facilitate the construction of Highway 401. Nowadays, the creek rises in a stormwater pond south of the highway at Terraview Willowfield Park and runs south for 16 kilometres through a cemetery, a golf course and Taylor Creek Park into the east branch of the Don River.

Heavily polluted by industrial runoff with its upper reaches encased in cement, Taylor Massey Creek is a sorry example of how low society can bring a once-luxuriant watercourse. That is, until it reaches Taylor Creek Park ravine, where it shakes off visual pollution to become something it used to be—a treat for the senses. Cattails line its marshy banks, red-winged blackbirds abound and dragonflies dart about, while in the reeds, small animals search out crayfish and look at people with pleading eyes.

The Don River

Although not a buried river, the Don is still a waterway of shame for what the good citizens of Toronto have done to it in the name of profit and convenience. During the 18th century, a gentleman immigrant to York needed only three things to succeed: a good wife, money and a river to power a mill wheel.

In 1795, Governor John Graves Simcoe granted success to the brothers Aaron and Isaiah Skinner by awarding them a section of pristine river at the town's eastern perimeter, which he had previously named the Don because its wide valley reminded him of the Don River in England. That land grant was for the construction of a lumber mill to supply York with building material, and the area was aptly named Don Mills. Deep and with a constant flow, the Don proved exceptionally well suited for driving water wheels, and its lower reaches soon attracted other industries: lumber, paper, breweries, distilleries, brick mills and quarries, and with the advent of steam power, slaughterhouses and chemical plants.

The wild upper reaches of the river were the realm of wolves, bears and bandits, such as the infamous Brook's Bush Gang of robbers and thieves. Its lower reaches, once pristine and teeming with fish, became an open sewer with effluent transported downriver into Ashbridge's Marsh, an unhealthy quagmire of bubbling sludge and stinking sewage. The Don became the city's working river and a convenient sewer for almost all of early Toronto's industry.

During the booming 1880s, the Don's lower reaches underwent straightening to provide dockage for more ships, but spring floods caused problems; a few years later, the river saw a hard right diversion along the concrete-lined Keating Channel into Toronto Harbour. During the early 19th century, the Don River hosted 31 separate sewage treatment facilities, 20 landfill sites for garbage disposal, and, in 1917, a huge garbage incinerator just north of Dundas Street East called the Don Destructor. This facility incinerated 50,000 tonnes of garbage annually for 52 years, dumping untold tonnes of heavy metals into the Don River.

In 1954, Toronto received the full brunt of Hurricane Hazel, and residents no longer wondered about the river's wide valley as the Don overflowed its banks, and floodwaters inundated the entire area. The Don drains water from 360 square kilometres of land that lies mostly within the City of Toronto through many tributary creeks that feed into three main streams, the East, West and Lower Don, with about 70 percent of the total flow coming from polluted storm runoff.

A sick river, the Don is ever so slowly being remediated through the efforts of citizens groups and a prodded-awake Toronto City Council, and sometime in the future the Don River may once again provide swimming holes for children and good catches for fishermen. However, even as the cleanup of the Don progresses, a new threat has arisen—the great 2.4-metre-wide Coxwell Sanitary Sewer, which gathers raw sewage from three-quarters of a million residents from Etobicoke to Downsview. The pipe transports wastewater to the treatment plant at Ashbridges Bay and is cracking badly and threatening to inundate the Don River with millions of litres of foul waste. Considering that the flow of crappy water in that pipe can be three times the volume of the Don itself, an outflow from the pipe could be devastating. The city has budgeted $30 million for a bypass that is currently under construction, while "people in the know" are keeping their fingers crossed that the fix will come in time and no more cracks will appear.

DID YOU KNOW?

Located across the river from the old Toronto Brickworks on Bayview Avenue, the Todmorden Mills, originally called Don Mills, was renamed Todmorden by local brewer John Eastwood because it reminded him of his hometown in Yorkshire, England. The area is now a heritage site where visitors can walk the same paths as Toronto's early industrialists did and tour a brewery museum, two of Toronto's earliest homes and the refurbished paper mill. It is a worthwhile tour, and participants are no longer required to hold their breath, as the Don River has undergone some remediation. During World War II, Todmorden Mills was the site of a military internment camp for German merchant mariners arrested in Commonwealth ports at the outset of the war. Those prisoners worked across the river at the Toronto Brickworks, and if visitors so desire, they may also walk the prisoners' path to drudgery.

KILLER WATER

The Devil's Christmas

On Christmas Day 1892, the conduit bringing clean water from the depths of Lake Ontario to the city pumping station at the foot of John Street broke and rose through the ice of Toronto Bay. By the time it was discovered, sewer-polluted harbour water had already inundated the city's water supply and would cause a massive outbreak of typhoid fever.

Wagons to the Rescue

On September 5, 1895, the conduit supplying the John Street pumping station broke in three places, but the damage was discovered early enough to close down the system. To keep residents supplied with water, the Street Commissioners Department hauled water from outside municipalities in trolleys constructed after the break of 1882. The horse-drawn trolleys travelling back and forth on streetcar tracks would transfer their cargo to horse-drawn street-watering wagons for distribution to residents. During the 45 days it took to repair the conduit, the city hauled and distributed almost 18 million litres of water.

MOLE CITY

On the Right PATH

Aside from Toronto's many kilometres of buried streams and creeks, there are more than 10,000 kilometres of sewers, untold thousands of kilometres of water pipes, subway tunnels, buried cables, numerous underground water reservoirs and the world's largest system of underground pedestrian tunnels called the PATH network. PATH is the city-financed guidance system that enables pedestrians to find their way through 28 kilometres of privately owned and maintained underground tunnels, with each PATH letter standing for a colour and direction: P is red and indicates south, A is orange and leads west, the blue T directs people north, and the yellow H points the way east.

Torontonians got their first pedestrian tunnel in 1900, when the T. Eaton Company burrowed under Queen Street to connect its main store with a bargain basement annex. *Good idea,* thought other companies, and by 1927, when the new Royal York Hotel tunnelled across to Union Station, about a dozen tunnels afforded pedestrians protection from adverse weather conditions.

This was small potatoes until the 1970s, when mole-hole construction clicked into high gear, and today, more than 50 downtown buildings, most of the city's tourist attractions as well as 1200 stores are connected by belowground passageways. People can duck underground and cheat the weather, shop, eat at dozens of restaurants, catch a subway at any of five stations or just stroll around from the northern limit at Bay and Dundas Streets to the Metro Convention Centre at the southern end.

LOST SUBWAY STATIONS

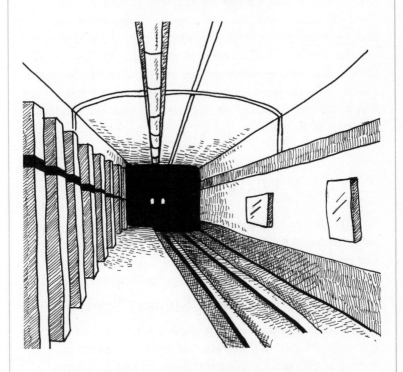

Lower Queen Street Trolley Station

On January 1, 1946, the citizens of Toronto decided through a referendum to build two subway lines—a train tunnel under Yonge Street to Eglington Avenue and an underground streetcar tunnel under Queen Street West. Workers set about constructing the subway train tunnel first, but not before building a starting point for the streetcar route. However, during that time, traffic had increased on Queen Street, causing the streetcar subway plans to be changed in favour of a sometime-down-the-road subway train route.

The Queen Street subway would be a constant down-the-road project for the TTC, and as late as 1966, it was still appearing on maps as a future line. It never was built, and today all that remains is that underground streetcar station lurking under the Queen Street Station like a rotten tooth. Subway riders using the Queen Station Station pedestrian underpass on the University line pass by a locked door that is an entrance to the spooky old station. According to newspaper reports, the abandoned station is a location for the latest remake of the slasher movie *Nightmare on Elm Street*. Freddy lives down there, and a look inside will make a believer of anyone.

DID YOU KNOW?

By 1909, the city had constructed about a half-dozen underground public lavatories with attendants counting more than one million uses per annum.

Lower Bay Street Subway Station

Originally part of the Bloor-Danforth line constructed in 1965–66, this station closed after six months of operation because of difficulties encountered while operating a reverse-direction crosstown line, the most important issue being a stalled train's ability to close down the entire TTC subway system.

Sealed up but not entirely forgotten, the Lower Bay Street Station was used by the TTC as a turnaround during 2007 repairs to the Bloor-Danforth line when train service was split at Museum and Osgoode Stations. During that time, passengers got a peek at the old station, with the TTC actually promoting it as a benefit of construction. This old subway station is supposedly haunted by a female spectre that TTC workers have dubbed "the woman in red" because she is always spotted wearing a long, red dress.

Disasters

Far more has been accomplished for the welfare and progress of mankind by preventing bad actions than by doing good ones.

–former Prime Minister William Lyon Mackenzie King

WAR AND DISEASE

During the city's formative years, surrounding forests pro-
vided cheap building materials for the construction of homes
and factories. The forests also provided firewood to heat those
homes and factories by rudimentary, mostly homebuilt
hearths and stoves. Fires occurred so frequently that when
Toronto was incorporated as a city, the first hundred or so
bylaws passed by city council were concerned with fire pre-
vention. It was a rare day or night in Toronto that some
building did not go up in flames, and with only water buckets
and hand pumpers, fighting them was near to impossible.

Fire was a constant threat and worry to residents of a city
constructed mostly of wood, as were diseases, especially
cholera and typhus, in a city growing through immigration.
Disease made the arrival of ships in harbour both a sweet
and a feared experience because they brought necessary
goods but sometimes death as well. Those worries aside,
early Toronto residents had another more ominous fear,
that of invasion from south of the border.

The U.S. Invasion

On April 27, 1813, U.S. forces occupied the city but suffered heavy losses as a result of the intentional detonation of Fort York's powder magazine. Enraged, the American invaders burned government buildings and looted the houses of officials. The citizenry demanded retribution, and while some historians point to this outrage as the impetus for the subsequent invasion and burning of the U.S. capital of Washington, that drive was more likely supplied by the burning of the undefended Lake Erie milling settlement of Port Dover during the spring of 1814. However, not all of York's residents suffered—a few offered the Americans assistance in the locating and looting of government stores and victuals. For help received, the traitors were rewarded with the stolen goods that were too heavy for transport—a vast quantity of agricultural implements, including ploughs and millstones. A later government search for those items proved fruitless, and only decades later was it learned they had been hidden in Lyons' Mill Pond, a dammed portion of the Rouge River owned by the miller John Lyons.

The Time of Cholera

It was the scourge of India—a disease of the small intestine caused by the bacterium *Vibrio cholerae*, a pathogen with a very short incubation period of just one to five days. Cholera has no hosts other than humans and is transmitted through a symptom of the disease, acute diarrhea, a condition that if left untreated quickly results in mortality through dehydration. Around 1800, the disease spread from India to Europe, reaching Britain in 1831 and arriving in Prescott, Upper Canada, the following year. Government officials instituted a policy of inspection and quarantine, but nothing helped, and the disease raged in both urban and rural areas. In 1832, cholera reached York, a ripe and ready city of 5000 people with open sewers and polluted drinking water. It killed about four percent of the population, an astronomical percentage that surpassed that of European cities, and the death rate might have gone higher had the city not been prepared with medical assistance and a quarantine program that included confining newly arrived immigrants in the Newgate Street cholera sheds at the city's eastern boundary. During the winter of 1832–33 the epidemic abated, and the citizenry of York thought their time of cholera had passed.

However, in the spring of 1834, with York celebrating its incorporation as the City of Toronto, ships arriving at the harbour with Irish immigrants brought cholera once more to the community. The disease was back, and though some historians blame Toronto's new, self-absorbed legislature for the ultimate gravity of the epidemic, no amount of preparation could have prevented the outcome because raw sewage inundated the city's entire water supply. This second cholera wave claimed over 1000 victims—20 percent of the population—an unprecedented figure equalling that of any disease-ravaged city of India. This final epidemic was a heads-up for city politicians, who almost immediately began planning a sewer and clean water system. While they awaited those improvements, Toronto's survivors wisely took to drinking beer instead of water and refrained from emptying their slop buckets into area creeks and streets.

UP IN SMOKE

The First Great Fire

In the early hours of April 7, 1849, Toronto's first Great Fire began in the city core at Post's Tavern, east of Jarvis and north of King Street. Volunteer firefighters from the city's four fire-halls were on the scene quickly and soon had water pouring onto the flames from fire hydrants installed in 1842. However, their gallant efforts were for naught as the fire had found fuel in the many wooden structures that surrounded buildings of brick and stone, and no amount of water could dent the ferocity of the blaze. The fire at Post's Tavern became a conflagration that spread to engulf the entire downtown area, destroying the original St. James Cathedral, the first city hall and a large section of the St. Lawrence Market. In a knee-jerk response to the disaster, Toronto City Council enacted a bylaw outlawing wood-framed structures, a law completely ignored both then and in modern times—even today, most of Toronto's houses are wood framed.

The Second Great Fire

On the cold and blustery evening of April 19, 1904, a Toronto constable noticed smoke rising from the elevator shaft of the E & S Currie necktie factory at 58 Wellington Street. Running to callbox 12, he called in the fire at 8:02 PM and returned to find the blaze well advanced. An hour later, every firefighter in Toronto was on site and battling fires on both sides of Wellington Street. By 11:00 PM, firefighters had stopped the blaze from spreading north, but high winds drove the inferno south and east into the Esplanade and to Front and Yonge Streets.

Responding to urgent telegrams, help arrived from outlying towns and the cities of Hamilton and Buffalo, New York. By 4:00 PM, some 250 exhausted firefighters had the blaze under control, but the devastation to the city's business and industrial section was absolute, with more than 100 buildings destroyed and 5000 employees out of work. A catastrophe, but with a fantastic ending—not one life was lost in the conflagration.

An interesting note is the callbox phone used by the constable to report the fire, as it became the everlasting name of the canteen truck servicing the needs of modern-day Toronto firefighters—Callbox 12.

A more important result of the incident is the long-time friendship that the blaze engendered between Toronto and Buffalo, which over the years has seen each city ready and willing to send aid during emergencies.

During Toronto's formative years, residents were required by law to keep two large water buckets in a handy location and respond immediately to the ringing of the St. James Cathedral tower bell that served as a fire alarm. Upon reaching a blaze, responders were to form a bucket brigade to the closest water source, which for many years was Toronto Harbour.

TWENTIETH-CENTURY CALAMITIES

The Spanish Flu Epidemic

Officially recognized at the Spanish town of San Sebastian in May 1918 and dubbed Spanish influenza, or the Spanish flu, the disease had already rampaged through the trenches of World War I battlefields, claiming thousands of victims. It arrived in Toronto in the early spring of 1918 via returning servicemen and immediately began decimating the population.

At the onset, Toronto doctors had no idea that they were dealing with a virus because the disease attacked people of all ages but killed mostly young adults between the ages of 20 and 30. Only later was this fact attributed to the virus causing a victim's immune system to release too many inflammatory mediators into the lungs, an unfortunate circumstance for those with strong immune systems. By midsummer, the flu had abated, and city health officials announced that the worst was over—a premature declaration because the disease returned in the early fall in a more lethal, mutated form.

The whole of Toronto was quarantined; churches, schools, theatres, shops, libraries and taverns all closed, and residents were not permitted to gather before or after funerals. The body count kept increasing, with streetcars pressed into service for corpse removal to mass burial sites. The Spanish flu killed an estimated 100 million people worldwide, with the mortality in Toronto estimated at 1200 to 1500.

The SS *Noronic* Fire

They called her the "Queen of the Lakes" and she was a beauty; at 110 metres in length with four cabin decks, the SS *Noronic* was one the largest steamers in Canada, and along with a crew of 200 could host 600 passengers. On September 14, 1949, the ship departed Detroit, Michigan, for a seven-day pleasure cruise that included two overnight stops in Canada before her return to Detroit. On board were 171 crewmembers and 524 passengers, mostly Americans.

On Friday evening, September 18, the *Noronic* docked at Toronto's Pier 9 terminal, at the place where the Westin Harbour Castle hotel now stands, and passengers embarked for a night on the town. At 2:30 AM, with the ship all quiet for the night, a lone passenger, Don Church, smelled smoke and followed his nose to a linen closet on C deck. Church summoned a porter, but they found the door locked, and the porter wasted precious minutes searching for the key. When the two men finally got the door open, the fire exploded into the hallway, enveloping the lemon-oiled walls. The pair tried to fight the flames with fire extinguishers that failed to work properly and fearing the worst, Don Church ran to his cabin on D deck, grabbed his wife and two children and departed the ship, fully expecting an alarm and a quick exodus of his fellow passengers. But that did not happen; the alarm system was broken and the telephone hookup to shore was unconnected. Crewmembers bolting from the ship failed to arouse sleeping passengers, and though a few crewmembers attempted to fight the flames, none of the vessel's fire hoses was operational.

At 2:38 AM, the ship's whistle sounded, but the *Noronic*'s decks were already half engulfed in flames. Rescuers arriving at the scene found the ship completely aflame and the dock filled with screaming passengers, some still burning. However, the worst was yet to come. Burning bodies began to rain down from the ship, and rescuers had to plunge into the harbour's icy water to recover the injured and the dead.

With few ambulances available at the time, taxis were pressed into service to transport the injured to area hospitals, and when those filled, the lobby of the Royal York Hotel became a temporary clinic. The morgue quickly filled to capacity, so bodies were transported to the Canadian National Exhibition's (CNE) Horticulture Building for storage. As many were completely incinerated by the intensity of the blaze, the death toll from the *Noronic* disaster is only an estimate—118 to 139 victims, all Americans and all passengers. An investigation found the cause of the fire to be a lit cigarette dropped by a crewmember in the linen closet. Blame was also attributed to the steamship company for having inoperative firefighting and alarm equipment and to the cowardice of the crewmembers. The steamship company in turn blamed the incident on arson, as another of its ships had experienced a similar linen closet fire.

Hurricane Hazel

They called the storm Hazel. It began life off the coast of Africa and blasted into the Caribbean as a full-blown hurricane, where it swept north up the Eastern Seaboard, losing strength and reverting to a tropical storm before turning eastward. Toronto reporters and radio announcers paid it little attention and downplayed the storm's ferocity as being just another bad weather day, as Toronto had already experienced several days of steady rainfall.

In the early afternoon of October 15, 1954, tropical storm Hazel collided with a strong western cold front before striking Toronto in late afternoon. Invigorated and back to hurricane strength, Hazel pounded the city with 110-kilometre-per-hour winds and a driving rain that exceeded 200 millimetres in less than 24 hours. With the ground already saturated from previous rainy days, runoff poured from streams, creeks, storm sewers and canals, inundating downtown Toronto at rush hour.

Chaos reigned as Yonge Street became a raging river that knocked down trees and power lines, carried away cars and flooded the subway at King Street. Toronto's two main waterways, the already overtaxed Humber and Don Rivers, flooded their banks, washing away bridges, houses, cars and anything in their paths. On Raymore Drive, south of Lawrence Avenue, Humber floodwaters carried away 14 homes, killing 32 people.

To the east, floodwaters turned the Don Valley into a scene of absolute devastation as debris dams formed and then let go, sending walls of water rushing downriver like battering rams. Don Valley bridges disappeared, homes lifted off their foundations and floated away, and industrial areas were flattened. Almost 2000 families found themselves homeless in a city that looked like it had been mauled by a monster.

The floods claimed 81 lives and became a heads-up for Toronto politicians, who immediately began drafting bylaws that would reshape Toronto by respecting the floodplains of its creeks and rivers.

DID YOU  KNOW?

The Bloor Street viaduct over the Humber River is marked by a slash of blue paint to indicate the height of the waterway during the Hurricane Hazel flood. You must look carefully to see it, but it is there, some 7.5 metres above the river.

The Toronto Islands

To put it [a red light district] in an area away from the city might make some sense, and the islands fit the bill. The industry exists and we're not making a penny from it.

–Councillor Giorgio Mammoliti

THE ORIGIN OF THE ISLANDS

A Sandspit in a Prehistoric Puddle

Old Lake Iroquois is best envisioned from atop the Scarborogh Bluffs, where the depth of that former glacial water body can be easily imagined by the height of the surrounding cliffs. These cliffs of clay are craggy because, exposed to the elements, they have been eroding into Iroquois's remnant puddle, Lake Ontario.

A mere shadow of its former self, Lake Ontario is still deep and restless because of the push of water from the Niagara River and the narrow outflow into the St. Lawrence. Fast currents abound in the waters of the lake, with the speedier ones able to carry eroded material from the Iroquois Escarpment for kilometres before throwing heavier bits out from the current and into piles. Sand is the heavy material, and the piles become sandbars that, depending on the turn of the current, can be almost any size and length. The current passing Toronto in earlier times saw a gentle push by the outflow of water from the Don River followed by another from the Humber, creating a long, curved sandbar and a protected bay.

When First Nations peoples first discovered the Humber River shortcut to Georgian Bay, the sandbar had become a spit with trees, grasslands and delightful beaches. First Nations travellers and fur traders called it the "Carrying Place" because paddling Lake Ontario in a birchbark canoe was such a dreadful undertaking that it was better to carry the canoe over the spit and paddle up the bay to the Humber River.

The Carrying Place had good air, the lake breezes being an important attribute for the Huron after they established a trapping settlement on the Humber River. It became their hospital, their place to recover from lake fever, a mild form of malaria.

From Sandspit to Islands

When the English arrived in 1787, they too recognized the healthy ambience of the spit, and it quickly became a place of recreation with access at first only by boat and a few years later by a bridge over the Don River and a road around the swampy Ashbridges Bay. That road made the spit easily accessible for carriage picnics and weekend riding excursions, but it also made the sand easily accessible to companies making bricks. Too much digging of sand from one spot weakened the spit, and, in 1852, high waves turned the peninsula into a real island. No problem—city authorities simply built a bridge and the picnics continued, as did the digging of sand to make bricks.

In 1858, another storm opened a huge breach and turned the entire spit into something resembling Swiss cheese. A natural calamity, but fortuitous for Torontonians in that it saved the peninsula from industry and allowed the Toronto Islands to become a place away from the industrial grime that would cloak the city for generations. From Governor Simcoe's wife, Elizabeth, we get a fine description of the spit that would become the Toronto Islands:

> *We are met with some good natural meadows and several ponds. The trees are mostly the poplar kind covered with wild vines and there are some firs. On the ground were everlasting Peas creeping in abundance of purple colour and pretty white flowers like lilies of the valley.*

A Bad Bargain

In 1787, when Lieutenant-Governor John Graves Simcoe decided to vacate Newark, modern-day Niagara-on-the Lake, for the more defensible Toronto, British law made it necessary to establish ownership through treaty with the indigenous peoples.

However, as the story goes, that proved difficult because the only indigenous folks the British could find were two families of Mississaugas passing through on their way to their camp by the Credit River. The British thought, *fine we will deal with them*, and so it was that the Mississauga band chiefs made their blots on a blank deed with the actual acreage to be filled in when the land was surveyed.

A dubious document even then, over the years the deed became even more suspect, and, in 1805, the British initiated a treaty redux with three Mississauga chiefs receiving 10 shillings each for re-signing the sale of 392 square miles (1015 square kilometres) of land. In 1998, the Mississaugas of the New Credit First Nation filed a claim for their property—all that Torontonians hold dear, including the Toronto Islands. It's a bit of a stretch, and though they will never win, they probably will receive a windfall of Canadian taxpayer's money for a fuddle-duddle treaty made by British politicos with people who had absolutely no concept of private property.

THE ISLANDS PEOPLE

Early Entrepreneurs

Despite being a one-time peninsula with a connection to the mainland past Ashbridges Bay marsh, the sandspit that forms Toronto Harbour has always borne the nickname "Toronto Islands" because it is so remote. During the city's formative years, road access to the peninsula depended on bridges constructed over the Don River that were prone to vanish during spring floods, making the area accessible only by boat and further perpetuating its remoteness. Around 1830, only the odd fisherman and a lighthouse keeper inhabited the Toronto Islands, and for that reason Benjamin Knott moved his malodorous soap and starch factory onto the peninsula narrows just west of Ashbridges Bay marsh. Called the Blue and Poland Starch Company, Knott's endeavour would be Toronto Islands' one and only factory, and it made Knott the only permanent inhabitant and a lonely man.

In 1833, ex-serviceman Michael O'Connor began advertising Toronto Islands' first hotel as a place for sportsmen, parties of pleasure and those wishing to inhale the healthy lake breezes. Who built O'Connor's hotel? The lonely Mister Benjamin Knott, and he built it right next to his malodorous soap factory. Not that it mattered, since his lessee Michael O'Connor had a liquor licence, sold good whisky at reasonable prices and always kept a baron of beef on a rotisserie to hide the rendering smells. O'Connor's Hotel became a popular spot for gentlemen seeking a few days of debauchery in a very remote location. This popularity caused the partners Knott and O'Connor to institute a ferry service from downtown to the narrows, a ferry powered by two horses walking on a treadmill that was connected to a paddlewheel.

In 1839, to escape the dreaded cholera, Governor General of Canada, Lord Sydenham, constructed a large summer residence at the narrows; when he died a few years later, Toronto retailer Louis Joseph Privet took over the house and, in 1843, opened his Peninsula Hotel. To attract paying customers, Privet installed several tame amusement devices: a bowling alley, a shooting gallery, a rudimentary merry-go-round, two tall swings and a small zoo. He called it the Peninsula Pleasure Grounds and provided ferry service from the city and a great wharf on which to unload passengers. In 1847, wheelwright Rueben Parkinson, attracted by Privet's action at the narrows, constructed his Parkinson's Hotel and would later construct another larger hotel on Centre Island.

Settlers Welcome

The 1840s marked a change of direction for the Islands. Up to its neck in infrastructure expenses, the city needed money and began looking at anything that might raise some funds. In 1846 when the Crown asked city council if they minded the Crown leasing some Island property to individuals, it was a wake-up call. Yes, the city did mind, and if anybody were going to lease land on the Toronto Islands it would be city council.

Okay, said the Crown, and, in 1847, they gave the city a "license of occupation." Although it did not give the city outright ownership, it was almost as good and triggered a race to get the Islands making money. By 1849, the city had laid out 50 large residential lots with streets named after British admirals.

Ferry Business

The 1850s brought even bigger changes to the Islands. In 1853, Louis Privet sold his hotel to John Quinn, who added a steam ferry and began substantial renovations. Unfortunately, his renamed Quinn's Hotel washed away in 1858 when a storm breached the narrows, creating the Eastern Gap and turning the peninsula into real islands. With no road access, the ferry business took off, and more steamers began to cross the waters of Toronto Harbour, bringing large crowds on weekends for bathing and picnics and to watch the sailing regattas and rowing races.

Tragedy Strikes

Around 1860, the Islands' healthy air encouraged David Ward to move his family from the city to the narrows, but on May 11, 1862, tragedy befell them when a sudden storm upset a small sailboat skippered by Ward's son, William, drowning the family's four young daughters. The remaining Wards moved to a site beside a small lake that became known as Ward's Pond, near to where his son William would construct the landmark Ward's Hotel in 1882, a pleasure palace that endured to the mid-20th century.

In 1865, another storm washed the home of narrows fisherman John Hanlan into the bay, carrying it all the way down to Gibraltar Point. Following David Ward's example, Hanlan abandoned the narrows and took up residence at the very western end of Centre Island, now called Hanlan's Point.

Carving Up the Islands

In 1867, just four days before Toronto's incorporation, the Crown gifted the city with clear title to the Toronto Islands. The city could finally start making some real money off the spit, and city council immediately conducted a survey, marking out 5-acre (2-hectare) lots, which they began leasing out in 1871 for $5.00 per year. Big lots begat fine homes that begat streets that begat more ferries that begat more visitors and places for them to stay overnight, such as Mrs. Parkinson's Hotel on Centre Island. Mrs. Parkinson would later sell out to the Mead family and the hotel became Mead's Hotel, famous for its scrumptious dinners. In 1880, the city leased a small island just east of Olympic Island to the Royal Yacht Club after its mainland club became untenable as a result of industrial encroachment along the waterfront.

The Islands' Favourite Son

Yachting was popular, but rowing had become all the rage world-wide. Weekend competitions held in the body of Islands water called Long Pond attracted large crowds of spectators, and they required policing. For that, the city hired John Hanlan as island constable in a deal that included a permanent lease on his west-end property, and, in 1874, Hanlan constructed a fine hotel on Hanlan's Point at the end of a great wharf.

John Hanlan had two sons; the youngest, Edward "Ned" Hanlan, was born to row, or more precisely to "scull," as that is what singles rowing is called, and there has never been another sculler like Ned. Two events put Canada on the world map, the battle of Vimy Ridge in 1917, and Ned's defeat of British champion William Elliot back in 1879. Ned Hanlan would become Canada's champion of champions, and his glory reflected onto the Toronto Islands, turning them into a place to go to watch Ned race and make history. The champion oarsman would be the catalyst of everything entertaining on the Toronto Islands. His racing abilities brought in crowds and forced the city to construct boardwalks and parks, and when Ned constructed a fine hotel with a small amusement park, that action would instigate the creation of the great Hanlan's Point Amusement Park.

 During most of the 19th century, the consumption of liquor and beer was verboten on the Toronto Islands as city officials tried to appease the temperance movement—a situation ameliorated by bootlegging hotel owners, including John Hanlan. Ned got in lots of midnight practice rowing over crates of whisky for his dad, and the police wanted him for bootlegging.

On a summer evening in 1876, armed with an arrest warrant, authorities raided the rowing club frequented by Ned and almost got him. However, alerted by the commotion out front, Ned slipped out a back window, commandeered a rowboat and headed out to intercept a lake ferry heading for the U.S. He was going there anyway, to Philadelphia, to compete in a great race that he won handily.

Ned's return to Toronto was that of a conquering hero, with the bootlegging warrant wisely plucked from police files by nimble-fingered politicians. Fired up by public adoration, Ned capitalized on both his popularity and apparent immunity from city liquor laws by constructing the 25-room Hotel Hanlan in 1880. His hotel featured plenty of amusements for guests, including dancing and vaudeville shows, and unlike mainland theatres, the liquor and beer always flowed at the Hotel Hanlan.

The Hotel Hanlan

In 1872, while his son Ned was making a name for himself in the popular sport of rowing, hotelier and Islands constable John Hanlan passed away in his sleep. Ned took over running the single-storey hotel with an idea to expand the facilities, but as the decade waned and his race winnings piled up, his idea turned to building a new hotel.

In 1880, the same year he beat Australian Edward Trikett for the world rowing championship, Ned cut the ribbon on the new Hotel Hanlan, a three-storey Victorian gingerbread confection complete with a ferry dock and a huge sign advertising his Coney Island–inspired carousel. Ned's carousel attraction was part of a small amusement park that over the coming years would expand into the huge and wondrous Hanlan's Point Amusement Park. Ned's Hotel Hanlan would survive fire and economic depressions and serve as the centre of Islands life until the building's demolition in 1966.

ISLAND LORE

Living on the Islands

Around the turn of the 20th century, the city banned tents at Hanlan's Point and campers moved to Ward's Island. In 1904, city workers counted 10 tent campers spending the summer on the island, but by 1912, that number had risen to 685 summer campers.

With returning World War II veterans encouraged to lease building lots on the Toronto Islands, by the early 1950s, the summer resident population had risen to more than 8000, with about 2000 living there year-round. Today's resident population, summer and year-round, is approximately 600 occupying 262 homes. Residents own their homes but lease their lots from the Toronto Islands Trust, the administrator of a provincial legislation called the Toronto Islands Residential Stewardship Act. Lot leases run until 2096, with the buying and selling of homes strictly controlled; residents may pass homes to spouses and children, but selling to others must be done through a public list.

DID YOU KNOW?

Back in 1950, a return ferry ticket to the Toronto Islands cost 14 cents. In 2010, the roundtrip fare was $6.50, and on the same ferry boats used in 1950. Go figure.

The Good Old Days

During the 1950s, the Toronto Islands consisted of three communities—Hanlan's, Centre and Ward's—with each island having a community centre, a sports team and a newspaper. Centre Island's "Main Street" featured several hotels, a dairy, a hardware store and a movie theatre.

Zipping Along

In the early years of the 20th century, Toronto Harbour would always freeze solid in winter, and ice boating was a favourite sport that sometimes saw hundreds of boats skimming around the harbour on weekends.

Everybody Skate

During the area's 18th-century tenure by the French, troops heading west from Fort Frontenac during winter were issued ice skates for travel on frozen Lake Ontario.

Leaky Accommodations

Upon their arrival at Toronto from Newark on July 30, 1793, Governor and Mrs. Simcoe set up house near the foot of present-day Bathurst Street in a large canvas tent purchased from the estate of famed British explorer Captain James Cook.

Not a Shot Fired

During the U.S. invasion of 1813, the shot from cannons fired from Fort York fell short of American ships, and the blockhouse constructed at Gibraltar Point on the western tip of the Toronto Islands never fired a single cannon. Why the blockhouse guns remained silent is a mystery, but it was probably thanks to their fixed train of fire on the harbour entrance. The blockhouse proved so militarily insignificant that it escaped destruction by the invading forces, an oversight corrected during the American's second unsuccessful invasion, in 1814.

Purloined Goats

Before the second U.S. invasion, a large herd of goats grazed the Toronto Islands, providing milk for city children. When U.S. forces departed the islands, they apparently took along the goats, as all the animals disappeared.

In 1883, the Lakeside Home for Little Children was constructed on the Toronto Islands for the summertime benefit of the city's many disease-afflicted youngsters. In 1891, newspaper publisher John Ross Robertson, whose daughter had succumbed to scarlet fever, built a huge addition to the Lakeside Home that featured an enormous veranda where the kids could get some fresh air. Every June, mothers and hospital workers would parade sick children from around the city down to the ferry docks for transport to the Lakeside Home. John Robertson was a generous man, and the kindness he showed to thousands of kids would see perpetuation as a wonderful institution called…the Hospital for Sick Children.

The Ancient Mariner

The Royal Canadian Yacht Club's renovated 20-metre-long ferry boat *Hiawatha*, built in 1855 at the Bertram Engine Works at the foot of Bathurst Street, is the oldest ship listed in Lloyd's Shipping Registry.

DID YOU KNOW?

The last massive flight of the now extinct passenger pigeon over Toronto occurred in the spring of 1876. Pigeons darkened the sky over the Toronto Islands and the city for hours, and estimates put their numbers at over 200 million. Roosting in the countryside, passenger pigeons were a prime target for area farmers, who used explosives to knock them out of trees. Stripped of feathers, the birds were pickled in salt, packed into barrels and shipped off to the U.S., where they sold for as little as a penny each.

Toronto Harbour

The waterfront is always in play. Toronto's basic geophysical bone structure is its river valleys and its waterfront, and its waterfront has always had a major role in determining its economy, its social life, its politics. It's always in play.

–former mayor David Crombie

THE WATERFRONT

In 1795, Governor Simcoe's wife, Elizabeth, noted in her diary that the waters of Toronto Harbour were calm and clear as crystal. A decade later, fishermen would set their nets in those calm, clear waters and haul up more than enough fish to supply the city's burgeoning population. Fish spawned in the marshes at the eastern end of the bay, but the dumping of mill effluent and sewage into the Don River soon turned the marsh into a putrid swamp where there were no fish. "That's the price of progress," was the mindset and the practice of unrestrained polluting of streams and creeks spread, with odious ramifications.

Completely enclosed except for the entrance channel and unable to cleanse itself with lake currents, Toronto Harbour quickly became a stinker, and after 1838, when the city began constructing sewers to drain indoor plumbing with conduits to Toronto Harbour, a super stinker. City council completely ignored the invasion of indoor plumbing that turned Toronto's many creeks and streams into open sewers and the harbour into a huge smelly cesspool. To placate residents who complained about the stench, city council began a process of converting streams and creeks into real sewers and constructing huge wharfs, beginning with the Queen's Wharf (at Bathurst and Fleet Streets) for the use of lake schooners displaced by sewer construction, with these eventually becoming quays to benefit larger steamships.

While this was happening, the harbour got a break when Fishermen's Island, at the bay's extreme east end, was breached during an 1852 storm, enabling the bay to clean itself via lake currents. A bit of dredging and infill created more waterfront called the Esplanade, which turned Toronto Harbour into an attractive proposition for shippers, especially after the railways chugged into town with cargoes of lumber and wheat, resulting in the construction of dozens of private quays. Toronto's waterfront became a hodgepodge of industrial buildings, shipping docks, passenger terminals, coal dumps, chemical plants and too many railway tracks, resulting in a drastic downturn in productivity that continued into the 20th century.

In 1910, the Toronto Board of Trade demanded that city council turn over the waterfront to a permanent commission for development, and, in 1911, the Toronto Harbour Commissioner Act was passed by the Ontario legislature, an act that provided for the appointment of five commissioners, three by the city and two by the Ontario government. Improvements to Toronto Harbour began almost immediately: Ashbridges Bay was drained, industrial sprawl was contained to eastern areas, tracks were sorted, the shore was cribbed by infilling and the harbour was dredged to allow for larger ships. By 1926, a half million tons of cargo arrived or departed from the harbour, and, by 1933, that tonnage had increased to two and a half million. Today, Toronto's harbour handles about a million and a half tonnes of cargo, almost all at the eastern end and out of sight of residents, while the western section, now called Harbourfront, has become more people friendly with walkways, parks and condominiums.

The Beginning

Steamboats brought prosperity to Toronto, the first being the Frontenac launched at the Kingston shipyard in 1815, followed by new launchings every year for decades. Not dependent on favourable winds, steamships enabled the creation of functioning timetables that increased trade with the U.S. and were convenient for passengers. However, sections of the St. Lawrence River remained unnavigable, making the transport of goods and passengers to the sea a halfway affair as steamships were forced to load or unload cargo at Kingston for haulage to or from Montréal by ox cart.

Then in 1824, the opening of the Lachine Canal enabled lake steamers to lock past the rapids and transfer cargo and passengers to or from ocean-going vessels. However, the next year, the Erie Canal opened, and while most goods arrived in Toronto through the Lachine Canal, most goods departed via the Erie Canal, especially from the west, as the Niagara River stopped up Great Lakes travel like a plug until the Welland Canal opened in 1829, precipitating a boom in steamboat construction.

By 1849, access to the sea from all the Great Lakes became a reality when the entire St. Lawrence River became navigable through the construction of new locks. Steamships could now travel from the lakehead to the sea and beyond, and western wheat farmers, both American and Canadian, breathed a sigh of financial relief. Into Toronto came the railways, bringing that wheat from both the American Midwest and the Canadian Prairie Provinces, and the shipping companies constructed great silos to store the grain and immense wharfs to handle ever-larger steamships. Private wharfs began to crowd Toronto's waterfront with start-up shipping companies forced to buy swampy ground at the harbour's east end for infilling.

Make Room for Trains

Toronto's waterfront was already chaotic when the railway arrived in the 1850s, turning the area into a nightmare for city council. With no alternative but to make some room, the city completely scrapped its long-time obligation to keep the waterfront for its citizens and began infilling the Esplanade to create space for what would soon be 16 railway tracks, several large and small depots, a locomotive round table, dozens of huge wharves, grain silos, an iron works and innumerable factories. Today, over 70 kilometres of railway tracks service Toronto Harbour, with the largest facility being Redpath Sugar Limited, manufacturing a half-million tonnes annually.

Black Lungs for All

Nowadays, city residents complain about the high-rise buildings blocking the waterfront, but back in the late 19th century, residents only saw the waterfront when the factories shut down on Sundays. The Esplanade became a financial cornucopia for a city council ruled for decades by the industrial and railway bosses, and whatever those bosses wanted, they got PDQ, while all their constituents got was more bad air.

Today, the city is famous for its many fine hospitals, most of which got their start treating the respiratory illnesses caused by foul air from the Esplanade. Envision the harbour in 1880, a dozen steamships spouting smoke, an equal number of trains with their stacks streaming soot, an iron smelter hardly visible through its haze, the Gooderham & Worts smokestack along with a dozen others belching particulates that covered the entire city in a grimy black dust. Doctors called it black lung disease, and while usually an affliction of coal miners caused by breathing coal dust, it was in Toronto like a plague and was usually diagnosed as chronic tuberculosis.

Waterfront Wonder

In 1913, the Toronto Harbour Commission began extending the waterfront 335 metres into the bay using the "Cyclone," the largest dredge in North America if not the world, and it lifted over 765 cubic metres per hour from the lake bottom onto both the Ashbridges Bay marshlands and the newly cribbed lakeshore. By 1917, more than 80 hectares of new land at Ashbridges Bay and 40 hectares at the lakefront were ready for new industry, and area hospitals continued their expansion.

Hoover and the Harbour

Toronto Harbour's ability to handle large ocean-going ships got U.S. Secretary of Commerce Herbert Hoover onside for the St. Lawrence Seaway Project. On a visit to Toronto in 1924, Hoover toured the harbour and announced to reporters that construction of the Seaway was inevitable. The "inevitable" took another 25 years, but in the end, Toronto's grimy waterfront benefited the entire nation—well, maybe not everyone, as the hospitals were still bursting at the seams.

The Big Squeeze

In 1959, to celebrate the opening of the Toronto Harbour Commission's new "Queen Elizabeth Docks" at the harbour's east end, the city got its one and only visit from an ocean liner, the *Queen Elizabeth II*.

Not a Ship to Be Seen

Nowadays, cars exiting the Gardiner Expressway pass by the front steps of the Toronto Harbour Commission, with their drivers giving no thought to the ships and yachts that once tied up there at the water's edge. The dozens of steamship wharves with their tall cranes are but a memory, and except for the raw sugar carriers at Redpath Sugar, people rarely see ships in Toronto Harbour. The great cornucopia that was once the source of the city's wealth has all but dried up, a victim of distance and the millions of trucks that now stupidly haul containers to the city from ports closer to the sea. As dumb as that is, the new system does have some advantages for Torontonians; the waterfront has once again become theirs, and all those famous hospitals are now running lotteries to stay in business.

Toronto Harbour has been infilled about 500 metres from its original shoreline, a fact that is apparent when looking at the Harbour Commission Building. Now occupied by the Toronto Port Authority, a federal agency, the building was constructed in 1917 at the water's edge to allow inspection boats to tie up at the front steps. Now high and dry, the building sits next to the York Street off-ramp of the Gardiner Expressway.

HARBOURFRONT

The Lamplighter Mystery

Constructed in 1808 by the Provincial Government of Upper Canada, the lighthouse at Gibraltar Point, Toronto's oldest surviving structure, was paid for by tolls levied on ships entering Toronto Harbour. It is also the site of a great mystery, that of the 1815 murder of its first keeper, John Paul Rademuller. Investigators surmised that he was killed by drunken soldiers for the rotgut whisky he distilled at the lighthouse; however, because no charges were ever laid, the crime remains a mystery.

Lost Opportunity

In 2004, a ferry service between Toronto and Rochester, NY, was instituted and then discontinued after only 11 weeks thanks to the lack of a passenger terminal in Toronto. The service tried again in 2005, this time with a proper Toronto terminal, but despite an impressive number of passengers carried, the service was discontinued in 2006 when the company lost funding from the City of Rochester after Toronto refused to contribute.

Ugly Stuff

Coal was king in Toronto until the mid-20th century, and ships' cargos were unloaded onto the waterfront in huge piles to be put onto trains for distribution to lakeshore industries and the yards of city coal distributors. Coal dust and soot covered the entire city. Until the advent of sand blasting in the 1960s, almost every building in the area was the colour of coal soot, the result of an almost century-long dependence on coal by industry and for home heating. That many city homes were constructed using yellow brick was a big surprise for residents.

Boaters and Parasols

From the 1890s to the 1950s, cruising the lakes was popular, and Toronto Harbour was the home port to many cruise steamships, including the 2000-passenger *Cayuga* that ran daily day-tripper excursions to Niagara Falls for over 50 years.

The Grand Hotels

Of course Toronto might as well be Buffalo, because we get each other's TV.

–Kevin McDonald, comedian

THE QUEEN'S HOTEL

From its beginnings as a seat of government, Toronto needed temporary housing for out-of-town legislators, and small hotels popped up to service that need. As the city grew in size, farmers supplying fresh produce and meats from the countryside had to find somewhere to overnight. A disparity of accommodations arose; Toronto's elite were hosted in comfortable hotels close to the town centre, whereas farmers found budget accommodations in saloon or tavern hotels near to Market Square, now the St. Lawrence Market area, or in outlying inns and taverns.

With the advent of steamship travel, the accommodation disparity continued, but with all classes of hotels concentrated around the lakefront wharves. The arrival of the railways during the 1850s brought a dramatic increase in the number of travellers and encouraged the construction of middle-class hotels close to rail junctions both in the city and in outlying areas. However, the city still lacked a palace, or grand hotel, that catered to the rich and famous. There was a hotel that catered to the famous, Frank's Hotel, located near Market Square, a favourite of travelling vaudeville performers, actors and theatre people, but it was known more for its haute cuisine, as its accommodations were not plush. The city also had a hotel catering to the rising middle class, Jordan's York Hotel, with good rooms and a marvellous cuisine. However, there was nothing for the rich until 1840, when lake boat owner Captain Thomas Dick constructed a group of three-storey commercial buildings at Front and Yonge Streets, which he called the Ontario Terrace.

Dick initially leased out parts to Knox Theological College and a furniture manufacturer, but, in 1843, he decided that his buildings would make a fine hotel. He kicked out the school and furniture company, spent a fortune remodelling and called his creation the Ontario Terrace hotel. The Terrace was Toronto's first "baby grand" hotel, which would eventually go through several name changes to become the magnificent Queen's Hotel.

The First Grand Hotel

In 1856, Captain Thomas Dick and Patrick Sword hired city architect John Howard to remodel a three-storey rowhouse hotel called the Ontario Terrace, which Howard had previously designed for Thomas Dick, into a hotel that they called the Sword. The partners would cater to a specific clientele, those out-of-town members of the Upper Canada legislature, and for that they ordered architect Howard and builder James Grand to spare no expense. The two obliged by adding an entire three-storey wing with a dining room and kitchen on the main floor, along with eight suites and 40 bedrooms on the upper floors, all with gas lighting and bathrooms. Opened on August 15, 1856, and considered a plush stay, the Sword proved an immediate success until the following year when the government moved to Ottawa.

With business falling off, manager Patrick Sword sold his share of the hotel to a J.B.J. Riley, who renamed it the Revere Hotel. In 1862, Riley sold his share to Captain Dick who renamed it the Queen's Hotel and dumped every penny he could borrow, beg or steal into the hands of city architects Gundry & Langly for a long-term renovation. Over the next few years, the Queen's would double in size, with a new east wing along Front Street, a renovation of the existing east wing to match, super-luxurious suites and a courtyard with an iron fountain and gardens.

Hotels are the heart and soul of any great city, and while Toronto was still far from great, in 1863, its heart and soul was in the Queen's, the city's first grand hotel. Guests arriving by steamship or rail were picked up at the wharf or station and could expect a hot bath waiting in their fine room, along with a wine and fruit basket. Captain Dick spared no expense in the kitchen, and a meal at the Queen's was something to write home about: moose, venison, wild turkey, lake trout, pigeon pie and the finest cuts of beef, lamb and pork.

The reputation of the Queen's Hotel spread far and wide along with the political views of its owner, Captain Dick. As a Southern sympathizer in the civil war raging south of the border, the good captain was not averse to lodging Confederate commercial and military agents under assumed names. During the American Civil War years, 1861 to 1865, the Queen's Hotel became a hotbed of intrigue, with its amenities shared by both Confederate provocateurs and Union agents. In the last year of the conflict, Captain Dick rented out almost the entire hotel to the Confederacy, and it became the South's de facto government headquarters.

Captain Dick died in 1874, and his great hotel passed into the hands of Dick McGaw and Henry Winnett, known historically as McGaw & Winnett, hoteliers. The pair got to work making the Queen's even greater through a redesign of the exterior that included dormers, a great rooftop cupola, extensive room renovations, a telephone in every room, central heating and Toronto's first elevator. By 1886, the Queen's Hotel could host 400 guests in first-class accommodations, or what management described as "isolated islands in the commercial sea of Toronto." The Queen's had become so highly regarded that when the Great Fire of 1904 threatened the hotel, employees volunteered to stand on the roof with brooms and water buckets to extinguish flying sparks, and guests hung wet bedsheets from every window.

The Queen's was a favourite of visiting royalty, and its register read like a who's who of the 19th century, but probably the weirdest and most noteworthy guests were the decade-apart visits of two main adversaries from the American Civil War. In 1868, after two years in a U.S. federal prison, former president of the Confederacy, Jefferson Davis, smuggled himself into Canada for a visit with exiled comrades in Montréal, Toronto and St. Catharines. In those cities, Jefferson was greeted by thousands of well-wishers who he would later call his lifesavers because they had rescued him from terminal despondency. In Toronto, he stayed at the Queen's Hotel in a suite ov erlooking the bay, dined nightly with old comrades and cried his eyes out when a band played "Dixie" on the hotel lawn. In 1881, Jefferson Davis' archenemy and the despoiler of Atlanta, General William Tecumseh Sherman of the U.S. Army, arrived at the hotel and stayed in, as legend would have it, the same suite overlooking the bay.

The St. Albans' Raid

On October 19, 1864, a group of 30 uniformed Confederate cavalrymen assembled on the Canadian side of the Vermont border and rode to St. Albans, Vermont, where they robbed a bank and tried unsuccessfully to burn the town. Chased back into Canada by outraged citizens, the group changed into civilian clothes and were arrested by Canadian authorities and held for extradition to the U.S. Extradition was refused, and the Confederates were released and allowed to keep the more than $200,000 in stolen bank loot. Several members of the released St. Albans raiding party were spotted some weeks later at the Queen's Hotel in Toronto celebrating their success with spymaster Captain Thomas Hines.

No Grief at the Queen's

When word reached Toronto of Lincoln's assassination, flags flew at half-mast, stores closed and churches held a special service, but at the Queen's Hotel, a special champagne celebration began early and lasted far into the night.

THE ROSSIN HOUSE HOTEL

The Rise and Fall and Rise Again of the Rossin

A few months before the Queen's Hotel opened for business, brickwork began on a hotel destined to be almost as grand an establishment. Conceived by brothers Marcus and Charles Rossin, successful Toronto jewellers, the five-storey hotel was designed and constructed by a U.S. company that employed novel building techniques. They used cast iron for fireproofing and exterior details, and the hotel had floor-to-ceiling second-storey windows. Aside from the fantastic windows, the second floor had almost 6-metre-high ceilings, a ballroom and several fabulous suites.

The Rossin House Hotel opened for business in May 1887 and, like the Queen's, she looked the epitome of 19th-century splendour, with a marble-floored reception area, Roman columns, palm trees, a grand staircase and ultra-comfy rooms. A jewel of a hotel, and as management liked to point out, almost fireproof.

However, "almost" only counts in horseshoes, and on November 2, 1862, the Rossin House Hotel suffered the humiliation of being gutted by a fire that left only the ironclad walls standing. The next day, owners Marcus and Charles Rossin beat it out of town, leaving the walls to the mortgage holder, James G. Chewet, a well-heeled elderly gentlemen not much interested in the hotel business.

The walls stood forlorn for two years while Chewet mulled over dozens of proposals to rebuild, with the commission finally going to the U.S. concern that originally constructed the hotel. In 1867, the Rossin House Hotel was back in business, and Torontonians could once again boast of having two grand hotels.

A Glimpse of the Past

During an 1856–57 bid to convince Queen Victoria to name
Toronto the capital of a united Canada, Toronto City Council
commissioned a photographic 360-degree panorama of the city.
Taken from the rooftop of the uncompleted Rossin House
Hotel at York and King Streets, the photographs disappeared
into the fog of history until found by a researcher in the
Library of the Foreign and Commonwealth Office in London,
England, during the late 1970s. Thanks to City of Toronto
Archives, those pictures may be viewed online by googling
"1856 Toronto panorama."

DID YOU KNOW?

In 1916, Russian revolutionary Leon Trotsky passed through
Toronto while on a tour of Canada to gather information about
what type of government Russia should aim for if his planned
revolution against the Tsarist monarchy should succeed. Although
no information about his visit to Toronto exists, he most likely
stayed at the Rossin House Hotel before continuing on to the
wild mining camps of Timmins and Swastika, where a record of
his three-week stay at the Swastika Inn does exist. In the spring
of 1917, on his way back to Russia by way of Halifax, Canadian
authorities detained Trotsky for several days before allowing him
to continue onward (to become second-in-command of the
Russian Revolution in October of that year).

THE ROYAL YORK HOTEL

New Kid on the Block

Around 1923, the once-glorious Queen's Hotel passed into the hands of the Canadian Pacific Railway, a company with designs on creating a flagship hotel in the "grand chateau" style promoted by their former president, Cornelius Van Horne. Their architects would be the team of George Allen Ross and Robert Henry Macdonald, the same duo that would design the future Union Station opposite the hotel.

In 1927, as the Queen's Hotel was coming down, both Union Station and a brand-new waterfront steamship terminal opened for business. However, arriving travellers looking for luxury were out of luck until June 11, 1929, when the grandest hotel in the British Commonwealth opened its doors to visitors demanding the finest of accommodations. At the Royal York Hotel, they got that and more—a lobby to rival any in the world, a bathtub and phone in all 1048 rooms and 10 elevators to get to those rooms.

THE KING EDWARD HOTEL

King Eddy the Great

Built by Toronto whisky distiller George Gooderham and affectionately known as the "King Eddy," the Kind Edward Hotel was an eight-storey affair designed by famed Chicago architect Henry Ives Cobb and the city's own E.J. Lennox, of old city hall and Casa Loma fame. *Ooh-la-la,* thought the city when the hotel's doors opened in 1903, and word got around to visitors that this was *the* place to stay in Toronto. Business was so good that in 1920–21, the hotel was reconstructed to 18-storeys and topped by the fabulous Crystal Ballroom. The finest rooms, deluxe bathrooms, a grand ballroom, marvellous dining, room service and afternoon teas that always included the world's best Parker House rolls—how could it not succeed?

Today, renamed the Le Meridien King Edward and completely refurbished, the hotel is once again back to being a grand place to stay while in Toronto and still offers diners the world's best Parker House rolls. Boarded up during the 1960s, the Crystal Ballroom is reputed to have a resident ghost, a fact unbeknownst to my brother and sister-in-law, who a decade later, got to use it as a venue for their wedding reception and were so happy that they probably didn't see the spook in the corner.

The Railways

Toronto is New York, as run by the Swiss.

–Peter Ustinov, actor

THE TRAINS

In 1793, Lieutenant-Governor Simcoe was so taken by the beauty of Toronto's lakeshore that he decided to preserve it from encroachment by reserving a 5-kilometre stretch as a common, or park. In 1818, the government of Upper Canada granted this strip of lakefront, called "the Walks and Gardens," to a committee of five public trustees and their heirs to keep it safe for future generations. In 1845, the city instructed architect John Howard to draw up plans for turning the hallowed public trust into a grand park. He released those plans in 1852, and the next year, the Provincial Legislature passed "The Esplanade Act," allowing the trustees of the Walks and Gardens to convey the land to the city for park conversion.

Big mistake that, because the Esplanade Act allowed the city a little leeway in regard to what was still a quaint form of transportation, the railway. Legislators probably imagined a solitary track providing access to the park for picnickers. What they failed to envision was how monstrously huge the railways would become and in so short a time. Nor did they predict how greedy Toronto City Council would become when it encountered the millions the railways had to spend on expansion.

In 1857, Toronto City Council convinced the provincial legislature to amend the Esplanade Act to allow them to sell off parts of the Walks and Gardens, ostensibly to raise funds for the landscaping of John Howard's lakeside park. That same year, trains began chugging into the Walks and Gardens, and Governor Simcoe's grand plan to preserve the beauty of the lakeshore was dead.

During the early years of the 20th century, with one fifth of Toronto's labour force employed by either the railways or companies servicing the railways, the city marched to the cadence of steel wheels. What the railways wanted they got, and they wanted to be as near as possible to shipping docks along the lakeshore. The Great Fire of 1904 provided space to construct one central depot destination for the more than 130 trains entering and leaving the city on a daily basis. That suited the railways, but the corridor of 16 tracks along the lakeshore, called The Esplanade, severely limited access to the lake by its citizens. The barrier turned dangerous as well, with hardly a week going by without a crossing accident or the crushing death of some child while scrounging coal.

By 1910, the many smaller railways servicing Toronto had consolidated through sales and mergers into three major players, the Grand Trunk, the Canadian Pacific and the 1880s brainchild of two city entrepreneurs William Mackenzie and Donald Mann, the Canadian Northern Railway. The big three railways ruled Toronto until the late 1960s, when industry began to leave the city for greener pastures. Gone but not forgotten, the railways left behind monuments of their rule—the Fairmont Royal York Hotel, the wonderful Art Deco Union Station and the vast marshalling yards that enabled the building of Toronto's most significant structures: the CN Tower, the Rogers Centre, the Air Canada Centre, the Metro Convention Centre and Roy Thompson Hall, among others. As a tribute to the rulers of the industrial age, the city saved the Canadian Pacific's roundhouse at John Street from the wrecker's ball and created the Toronto Railway Heritage Centre.

Moving Iron

Established in 1851, the Ontario, Simcoe and Huron Railway imported its first locomotive from the U.S. with the James Good Locomotive Works at Queen and Yonge Streets constructing subsequent engines. Moving locomotives from the factory to the rails on Front Street became a five-day attraction for city residents, with hundreds gathering to watch the 30-tonne behemoths creep down main streets while workers leapfrogged the iron rails.

The Way Across

In 1855, the Great Western Railway (GWR), Ontario's first rail network, built the great Niagara Falls Suspension Bridge across the Niagara River, enabling the transport of freight and passengers from Toronto to New York City.

On March 12, 1857, a Great Western Railway train travelling from Toronto to Hamilton broke an axle while crossing the Desjardins Canal bridge into Hamilton and plunged into a frozen canal, killing 60 passengers. Ironically, one of those fatalities was the man responsible for halting what had been a mandatory inspection stop by trains before crossing the canal bridge.

Royal Thrills

In 1860 during a royal visit, Edward, Prince of Wales, took a railway journey from Toronto to Collingwood. On the return trip, with the prince urging the locomotive engineer to keep throttling up, the train attained an unheard of speed of 55 miles (90 kilometres) per hour.

The Quick Way

During the 1860s, 90 percent of the grain from the American Midwestern states moved through Toronto on its way to U.S. Eastern Seaboard ports.

Complaint Department

The most frequent complaint of train passengers during the 1870s was their inability to see anything but thick forest out the windows. This situation was soon remedied because early steam locomotives burned massive amounts of wood.

On the Lake

In 1873, the second Union Station opened on the waterfront west of York Street with its grand Italianate façade and entrance facing the lake rather than Front Street, as most train passengers, including many thousands of immigrants, arrived by steamship.

An Unfortunate Occurrence

In 1873, Mister John Sheddon, president of the Toronto and Northern Railway was crushed to death by one of his own loco-motives. To honour his tenure, the company named its first bi-directional locomotive, the "Sheddon." The next year, while taking on water at the company's Stouffville station, the Sheddon exploded, killing the engine crew.

Tit for Tat

In 1876, Toronto's *Globe* newspaper chartered a Great Northern Railway train for morning runs through southwestern Ontario to deliver its newspapers. *Globe* publisher and Father of Confederation George Brown had a special affinity with the Great Northern because selling the company firewood from his estate had kept his newspaper solvent for years.

High and Dry

In 1887, the CPR opened its John Street roundhouse on land reclaimed from the harbour. Today, the roundhouse is both a museum and an artisanal brewery, but constant infilling has put the structure far away from the lake it once called home.

A Premature Service

In 1892, the Grand Trunk Railway initiated a commuter service to its various stations but discontinued the run a few years later because of a lack of interest. Toronto would not see another com-muter rail service until 1967, when the GO Transit Lakeshore went into service.

As Good as Gold

In 1884, the Canadian/American Express Company constructed a depot at the second Union Station for the transport of valuables in sealed railcar compartments. Purchased by the Grand Trunk Railway in 1892, the American Express business became the Canadian Express service, giving that railway an almost complete monopoly in the transfer of valuable cargo such as gold currency and bullion.

Theirs Becomes Ours

By 1913, passengers could get to the west coast on the lines of a half-dozen separate railway companies that depended on immigrant traffic and British investment money to stay in business. The next year saw the start of World War I, and with both sources of railway support suddenly dried up, the railway bosses turned to the Canadian government for financial assistance. A big mistake because it exposed their precarious financial situations, prompting the government to initiate the 1918 to 1923 cobbling of the half-dozen companies into a national conglomerate they called the Canadian National Railway (CNR). To appreciate the size of this new railway concern, one only has to think of its roster of 3256 locomotives in 1919.

A Spider Web

In 1917, Toronto was serviced by nine railways with terminals in the city: the Grand Trunk Railway, the East and West Grand Trunk Railway, the Southern Midland and Northern Railway, the Canadian Pacific, the Toronto Grey and Bruce Railway, the Hamilton and Buffalo, the Hamilton and Quebec, the Sudbury Toronto Ottawa Railway and the Northern Railway.

No More Coal

On August 26, 1929, Torontonians attending the CNE got their first look at a diesel-powered locomotive when the CNR moved engine No. 9000 onto a display track.

THE TROLLEYS

No More Muddy Boots

In 1849, a city furniture maker and undertaker named Henry Williams decided to use his construction abilities and livery horses to haul living people. He built a small, four-passenger omnibus that ran back and forth from Market Square in the St. Lawrence Market district to the Red Lion Inn on Yonge Street in the community of Yorkville.

For the next decade, things went well for Williams, and he added more trolleys, including a 10-passenger omnibus, but, in 1861, his fortunes took a downturn when Alexander Easton breezed into town from Philadelphia with a proposal to put horse-drawn busses onto tracks, something he had already accomplished in two American cities.

Toronto City Council took a shine to his idea, dumped Williams and awarded Easton a 30-year omnibus franchise for an unincorporated company he called the Toronto Street Railway. On September 10, 1861, Torontonians gathered along the length of Yonge Street to cheer as Canada's first horse-drawn omnibus on tracks trundled down to Market Square. The next year, there were two more routes in operation: Bloor to King Street, and Queen Street to what is now Ossington Avenue.

DID YOU KNOW?

The last excursion by a horse-drawn streetcar occurred on August 31, 1894, on McCaul Street, a hardly noticeable change as, even today, city streetcars plod along as if pulled by horses.

Trolleys North

On March 2, 1877, Robert Jaffray, a wealthy city grocery retailer and former member of the Royal Commission investigating northern railways, convinced the Ontario legislature to grant him incorporation for a street railway to run north of the town of Yorkville. Jaffray sold shares to investors and, calling his incorporated company the Metropolitan Street Railway Company of Toronto, instituted a horse-drawn omnibus service on Yonge Street north of Scollard into the suburbs. The next year, the Metropolitan laid rails to other suburban areas, giving the city a multi-destination, interurban tramway for which the company received a 30-year franchise.

In 1880, the brothers Charles and William A. Warren bought an interest in the Metropolitan, ostensibly to run a service to their property in Glen Grove, a small rural community north of the city, where they intended to set up a trolley park and sell building lots. Like Robert Jaffray, the Warren brothers had made their fortunes in the grocery business, but unlike Jaffray, who was more interested in politics than running a trolley company, the brothers had no interests outside of making money. Money makes money, and the brothers gathered all they could, bought out Jaffray and took on a new 30-year city franchise, calling it the Toronto Street Railway Company. By 1891, their cars were carrying 55,000 passengers per day over 110 kilometres of track in 350 cars, 50 busses and 100 sleighs pulled by a stable of almost 1400 horses.

Business was booming, but beginning in 1883, the brothers Warren, especially William, started to watch the goings-on at the Canadian National Exhibition grounds, where John J. Wright, an Englishman living in Toronto and Philadelphia, Pennsylvania, was conducting electric-motor trolley-car experiments.

Wright's first effort to move a railcar using an electric motor had been a bust when, in 1883, the car had refused to budge more than a few metres in front of thousands of CNE spectators.

Undaunted, he returned to the drawing board, and his demonstration at the 1884 CNE was better, but still unimpressive.
In 1885, he was back, having invented a new way to supply
electricity to the railcar's motor through an overhead wire with
a pole connection. His electrified streetcar worked like a dream
and hauled around more than 50,000 CNE patrons and the
Warren brothers.

By 1890, people attending the CNE could arrive there by
a Toronto Street Railway Company electrified streetcar from
almost anywhere in the city. However, in 1891, the Warren
brothers and the company's board of directors called it quits as
the 30-year city franchise had run its course. They simply stopped the
trolley service, forcing the city into an arbitrated settlement of
$1.5 million, after which the city found itself in the trolley busi-
ness. Not for long, however, as three months later, the city awarded
a 30-year franchise to George Kiely, the former vice-president of
the Toronto Street Railway Company, and railway entrepreneur
William Mackenzie with the conditions that the $1.5 million
arbitration money be paid back over 30 years and the city get
a piece of the action.

Agreeing to those terms and calling their new acquisition the
Toronto Railway Company, Kiely and Mackenzie immediately
set about replacing their horse-drawn rolling stock with the
new electrified versions, a feat they accomplished by the end of
1892. The company flourished but, because of its 30-year tenure,
refused to lay new track into expanded areas of the city, an atti-
tude backed up by the Privy Council in England. In 1911, the
city formed the Toronto Civic Railway and began to lay their
own track, an action that set the stage for the 1921 takeover of
the Toronto Street Railway Company routes and establishment
of the Toronto Transportation Commission, which in 1954
would become the Toronto Transit Commission, or TTC.

Horsey Heaven

The Toronto Street Railway Company constructed a new horse barn in 1886 at 165 Front Street East. The red brick heritage building is still standing and is presently used as a theatre.

According to a rule in its franchise, the Toronto Street Railway Company was required to maintain wintertime operations by clearing snow from tracks. The company employed horse-drawn ploughs and that worked well, except in downtown areas where they ticked off local merchants by throwing snow onto sidewalks. In February 1881, after a heavy snowfall, shop hands and merchants furiously attacked the ploughed snow, shovelling it back onto the tracks. The battle lasted for several days, with both sides improving their technique, the ploughs taking a galloping run and the merchants heaping on heavier, wetter snow. In the end, the merchants succeeded in entombing a plough in snow, and the TRC threw in the towel and agreed to supply men to shovel walks alongside their ploughs.

Cheap Thrills

In the latter part of the 19th century, touring the trolley circuit was a favourite pastime of Torontonians. Buying a quarter's worth of tickets enabled a 65-kilometre uninterrupted ride around the city, with passengers able to get off and on again anywhere they pleased.

Trolley Fun

At the beginning of the 20th century, hired or private trolley cars became popular, especially "moonlight excursion cars" that were decked out with coloured electric lights like rolling Christmas trees. These trips were lots of fun, and a few dollars slipped to the motorman would blind him to the odd keg of beer hoisted onboard.

Going Underground

The 30-year franchise awarded to the Toronto Street Railway Company gave the business exclusive rights to operate all surface transportation. In 1912, an American engineer submitted a proposal to city council that would circumvent that exclusivity by building a Yonge Street streetcar route underground—a good idea not acted upon for another 42 years, when the TTC began construction of the Yonge Street subway.

Dangerous Travel

In the early years of the 20th century, Toronto was a spider web of iron rails used by speeding trains and streetcars, with calamitous meetings of the two almost unavoidable. Trolley and train collisions would see the wooden streetcars splintered into pieces with their passengers killed or seriously injured.

No Sale

In the early 1920s, North Americans travelled mainly by train or streetcar as only a small percentage owned automobiles.

Bent on change, the big automobile companies instituted a relentless campaign to get people off the rails and into cars. One of that era's most nefarious "dump the trolley" projects, the brainchild of General Motors, was called National City Lines, a company that bought controlling interest in over 80 U.S. city rail companies and then systematically dismantled their operations. The overtures to buy Toronto's antiquated street railway system made by General Motors of Canada to city council served as a wake-up call to officials that their streetcar system was in need of a complete overhaul.

Trolley Mix

Prior to the 1921 takeover by the TTC, the Toronto Railway Company employed a fleet of around 60 electric trolley cars, including some manufactured by the Preston Car Company, Niles Car and Manufacturing Company and the Birney Safety Car, manufactured by the J.G. Brill Company in Philadelphia. After the takeover, the TTC switched to an electric trolley car designed by Peter Witt—Cleveland, Ohio's, transit commissioner—and manufactured by the J.G. Brill Company. Between 1921 and 1923, the TTC acquired 525 Peter Witt–designed electric trolleys, with some remaining in service until 1962.

Going Modern

In 1929, to counter rider erosion by the automobile, the American streetcar and trolley industry formed the Electric Railway Presidents Conference Committee, a group of company engineers and designers charged with reengineering and redesigning streetcars to make them more efficient and user friendly.

In 1931, the group unveiled their creation in Chicago to rave reviews. Called simply the Presidents Conference Committee Car, or PCC, the metal cars were longer, faster, more streamlined and more comfortable and came with air-operated brakes and doors.

The City of Toronto ordered 140 cars in 1938 and embarked on a program to replace its fleet of aging streetcars. Over the next decade, the city bought another 400 PCC cars built jointly by the St. Louis Car Company and the Canadian Car and Foundry in Montréal. During the 1950s, the city added another 205 used PCC cars bought from companies going out of business, bringing its total fleet strength to 745. These PCC cars served the city until the 1970s, when the Ontario government instituted another design conference that came up with the Canadian Light Rail Vehicle so familiar to modern-day Torontonians.

Selling Trolleys

In 1966, the Toronto Transit Commission, once a buyer of used trolley cars, became a seller when they unloaded 139 of their oldest PCC cars onto the city of Alexandria, Egypt.

The Amusement Parks

If it's decided by politics, Beijing will get the vote [for the 2008 Summer Olympic Games] on July 13. If you ask the wives where they want to go, it's Paris. If you ask the athletes, it's Toronto.

–former mayor Mel Lastman

IDYLL ON THE ISLANDS

A Summer Escape

Summers in 19th-century York were hot and sticky, and the social requirements of wearing woollen clothing made city life a misery for residents. Cotton was for undergarments, and if a constable caught anyone wearing undies for a swimsuit, that person would be arrested and dragged in front of a magistrate. To avoid woolly summers, residents took to places that had no constables: sailing on the bay or camping out on Toronto Island.

In 1843, to accommodate visitors to the island, brothers Joe and Peter Privat constructed a small hotel along with a few entertainment devices to amuse their clientele: a small carousel-type ride, a set of tall swings, a 10-pin bowling alley and a tiny zoo. Toronto's sandy peninsula was a popular summer destination for city dwellers until 1858, when a violent storm turned it into multiple destinations called the Toronto Islands.

The Beaches

In the confusion, the whole of Toronto took to their horses and buggies and headed east down the long trail past Ashbridge's Bay to an area called The Beaches. Sensing opportunity, local landowners began to subdivide their properties for the construction of summer homes and private promenades and beaches such as Balmy Beach Park.

In 1875, a horse-racing track called Woodbine Park began to draw so many Torontonians that the Toronto Road and Concrete Company did something truly innovative for the times by constructing a concrete tramway so folks could leave their horses at home. They called their service the Kingston Road Tramway, and, in 1878, with tramway service to the gate and a steam ferry from the city several times a day, Victoria Park opened for picnics, badminton and bike riding. The Scarboro Heights Hotel opened that same year. The trolley line prompted other private parks—Kew Gardens and Munro Park—to sprout up, and when a few streets were constructed, the summer communities of Woodbine, Kew and Balmy Beach were established. The Woodbine Riding and Driving Club racetrack became Woodbine Park and, along with the Woodbine Hotel, provided Torontonians with more reasons to head to The Beaches, as did the electric streetcars of the Toronto Railway Company.

More Fun for Everyone

The summer of '85 saw Woodbine Park host Buffalo Bill's Wild West Show, starring Annie Oakley and Chief Sitting Bull, and the three-day spectacle hooked Torontonians on summertime entertainment with frills and thrills. Staid at first, the trolley park frills consisted of non-alcoholic refreshment stands, band concerts, Punch and Judy shows, lawn bowling, cycling and tennis, with the thrills provided by a promenade or swim in cotton undies. Heady stuff, but whispers of greater thrills drifted up from New York City, and Torontonians began to pine for a place called Coney Island, with the musical roundabout of racy wooden horses they called a carousel.

Woodbine Park had real racehorses and the eastern beach "trolley parks," so called because residents reached them by TRC electric trolleys, stuck with their rather tame entertainment, but back in town, things were happening on the Toronto Islands.

The city had leased out cottage and camping lots, instituted a regular ferry service and constructed a promenade boardwalk and gardens, and several fine hotels were in business: Pierson's, Ward's and Hanlan's Hotels, the latter built by John Hanlan, father of world champion sculler and major island attraction Ned Hanlan.

With his rowing career going full tilt, the worldly Ned Hanlan took over management of the hotel after his dad passed away and began to look around for something to replace the excitement created by his famous rowing matches. Using his considerable winnings from rowing contests, Ned built a new Hanlan's Hotel along with garden walkways, swings, a bowling alley and a beach for swimming. Staid stuff for the worldly Hanlan, and around 1887, he gave over the running of the hotel to the Dotey brothers who operated the ferry service to the Toronto Islands and were already involved with setting up amusements devices at Hanlan's Point. Sensing what people really wanted at trolley parks, the Dotey brothers would, over the coming years, install many thrills and a baseball stadium on their leased property in a project to be called Hanlan's Point Amusement Park.

Losing market share to Hanlan's Point's growing list of amusements did not sit well with the new owners of The Beaches' tram service, the Toronto Railway Company, who by this time had taken over the eastern promenade trolley parks. In 1905, the TRC paired with property developer Harry A. Dorsey in a plan to develop an amusement park modelled after Luna Park at Coney Island. Dorsey bought 16 hectares of land plus 10 hectares of waterfront lots from the Sisters of St. Joseph, and the TRC helped him raise over half a million dollars to finance the park's construction.

On Saturday, June 1, 1907, Scarboro Beach Amusement Park opened its doors offering the public over 100 attractions. There was something for everyone: thrill rides, carousels, dance halls, bandstands, freak shows, funhouses, refreshment stands, games of chance, a boardwalk and even change houses for swimming in undies. In 1913, the TRC bought out Harry Dorsey and took full ownership and operation of the hugely successful amusement park, while in the city, jealous businessmen and politicians were already discussing ways to undermine that success.

WHOLESOME FUN

Swim 'n' Suds

Toronto's fascination with amusement parks began after 1830, when Joseph Bloore dammed Rosedale Creek to run the mill at his new brewery. The dam created a lake that soon became popular for swimming in summer and ice-skating in winter. Bloore's brewery was the city's first popular family attraction, and beer drinking was encouraged.

Summer Hill Park and Pleasure Grounds

In 1853, Charles Thompson's livery business began to suffer from streetcar and railway competition, so he opened his house, called Summer Hill, and its 80 hectares of grounds to the public for paid admission to what he called the Summer Hill Spring Park and Pleasure Grounds.

Thompson's home, just north of Bloor Street, between Young and Mt. Pleasant Road, was convenient for city residents and became popular after he installed tall swings, games and a diving board for people wanting to swim in his pond. His park was well liked, but the next year, when he converted the bottom floor of his home into a dance pavilion, it became a sensation. While the band played on, patrons danced the night away or stood and watched as they munched on delights prepared in his kitchen. Charles Thompson made a small fortune from his picnic grounds and dancehall and lit the fuse for Toronto's coming love affair with amusement parks.

Woodbine Park

In 1875, sensing an opportunity afforded by the Kingston Road Tramway extending its service into the eastern beaches, William J. Howell, proprietor of a Yonge Street saloon called the Woodbine Tavern, purchased 38 hectares south of Kingston Road for the construction of a racecourse. He called it the Woodbine Riding and Driving Club, but patrons called it Woodbine Park. Although it remained a rudimentary endeavour for years, Woodbine Park began to come alive when the Kingston Road Tramway Company, soon to be taken over by the Toronto Railway Company, ran a horse-drawn tramway past the entrance. The resulting upsurge in attendance enabled Howell to host spectacular racing events. By 1885, he had rebuilt the racecourse into so popular a spot that Toronto businessman Joseph Braun constructed a fine hotel near the racetrack. In that year, Howell's refurbished park hosted a marathon three-day Buffalo Bill's Wild West Show with Annie Oakley and Chief Sitting Bull wowing the huge crowds. The show was a financial windfall for Howell and pointed the way to a future for non-horsey events at the park. Woodbine Park began hosting dog and bike races, steeplechases, pigeon shoots, company picnics and polo matches. In 1888, Howell leased the track to a syndicate of investors calling themselves the Ontario Jockey Club, and in collusion with the Toronto Railway Company, the Jockey Club began hosting annual race meets at Woodbine Park.

Kew Gardens

Prompted by William Howell's up-and-coming Woodbine Park racecourse project and the Kingston Road Tramway, The Beaches farmer Joseph Williams installed cottages and camping accommodations along with several amusement devices, and, in 1879, he opened his lakeside property, which he named Kew Gardens Park, for what he advertised as "innocent amusement without spirituous beverages."

Hearty farm-style meals were available to patrons, along with iced buttermilk and fresh fruits from Williams' orchards. When not stuffing themselves with country cooking, visitors played baseball and tennis, rode bikes, watched Punch and Judy shows or sat and listened to band music. Come nightfall guests would sit around bonfires singing songs while munching peanuts and popcorn. Pretty tame, but on weekends, the park would sometimes host a thousand visitors, with almost all arriving and departing via horse-drawn tramway. In 1907, the City of Toronto bought Kew Gardens Park, and after razing all the buildings, they turned it into a public park.

DID YOU KNOW?

In 1859, the Toronto Islands ferry steamer *Firefly* began making Tuesday and Friday evening moonlight excursion around the bay with a band supplying music for dancers. The following year, the Carlton Park Race Course, a track built by Toronto lawyer W.C. Keele, opened along the West Toronto concession road, now called Keele Street. The first Queen's Plate took place there on June 27 of that year.

Glen Grove Park

In 1886, Charles Warren, president of the Metropolitan Street Railway Company, established a trolley park at Glen Grove, a rural community north of the city that today is the Lytton Park area. Warren's trolley park featured a horse-racing track and playing fields for various sports. However, the main goal of this endeavour was to sell subdivided portions of the property for home building, with the park eventually being sold out of existence. While never important as an entertainment centre, the quick turnover of Glen Grove Park into a subdivision was a lesson in the power of tramways to future property developers and the Toronto Ferry Company.

Victoria Park

In 1877, a syndicate headed by Toronto land speculator John H. Boyle leased 5.5 hectares of forested lakefront property from city merchant Peter Peterson for the construction of an amusement park to be called Victoria, because they planned to open by Victoria Day 1878. On that date, Victoria Park, under the management of brothers James and Thomas Gardiner, opened to rave reviews in every newspaper.

The Gardiners, ostensibly working for the Boyle syndicate but probably already in the employ of the forward-thinking Toronto Railway Company, left the forest intact for nature enthusiasts to hike, and their installation of a giant observation tower for those not inclined to walk through the woods provided a bird's-eye view of the entire area and the city. The brothers also built a wharf, enabling Torontonians the luxury of arriving by lake ferry rather than the cramped and slow horse-drawn tramcars.

By 1892, with the TRC's new electric tramcars stopping at the gate, the park went into higher gear and featured a steam-driven carousel, ultra-high swings, donkey rides, band concerts, a shooting gallery, acrobats, high-wire acts and, in 1897, a chance to explore the remains of the *Zebra*, a lake steamer fortuitously blown onto the park's beach. Visitors wishing to camp in style could rent one of 13 retired and refitted horse-drawn TRC tramway cars situated in various parts of the property.

In 1899, Victoria Park was purchased by Toronto brewer, land speculator and city alderman Thomas Davies, who announced that he would subdivide the property for homebuilders. However, that never happened, and the TRC ran Victoria Park until it was sold at auction in 1906 to Henry P. Eckardt, a city grocer and local landowner. That was the end of the park, but, in 1912, Eckardt allowed the Toronto Board of Education to use 6 hectares of the property for its famous "forest school," an outside summer learning camp for nature-starved city kids. Good for the kids and good for the TRC, because, along with the brothers Gardiner, it could now concentrate all its resources on its bigger source of income…Munro Park.

BRING ON THE RIDES!!!

Munro Park

Torontonians loved to dance, and in 1886, the TRC obliged them by opening another trolley park. For dance expertise, the TRC hired dance hosts from the ferry boats that had been offering moonlight dance excursions on Toronto Bay for years. The hosts knew that dancers loved waxed hardwood floors, and that's what patrons got at Munro Park's fantastic 1300-square-metre dance pavilion, along with paved walkways to keep their shoes clean and dry. They also got free mineral water at intermission from the park spring to reinvigorate flagging spirits, as real spirits were verboten at TRC trolley parks.

In 1896, the TRC effectively took control of all the trolley parks when they assumed the management of Victoria Park. In 1898, the TRC installed something for non-dancers at Munro, a 150-foot-high Ferris wheel, and a fabulous carousel began to merrily go 'round. Families had never had it so good, and if they were not riding the rides, they were walking the boardwalk trying their hand at the many games of chance and dodging jugglers and acrobats, while overhead, tightrope walkers performed death-defying feats.

In 1900, Munro Park introduced patrons to the wonder of motion pictures, and three years later, there were minstrel and variety shows, a lion tamer and daily hot-air balloon ascensions, weather permitting. In 1906, with the lease set to expire on the park, the TRC had already prepared itself for a change of venue.

DID YOU KNOW?

The fresh-air "forest school" established at Munro Park in 1912 followed a concept that originated in Germany in 1904 to counter the ravages of tuberculosis (TB) on children. Adherents believed that bad air caused TB, and keeping children outside in fresh air would counteract the disease. The concept became popular in Toronto and was adopted by the regular school system to benefit kids exposed to TB. Children attended classes in regular schoolrooms, with windows left wide open in all weather. To keep the kids warm, the city's education department supplied specially made blanket coats that covered them from head to toe.

Scarboro Beach Amusement Park

Modelled after Luna Park at Coney Island, Scarboro Beach Amusement Park opened on Saturday, June 1, 1907. Ostensibly under ownership of Toronto businessman Harry A. Dorsey and managed by the Gardiner brothers, the park, with its more than

100 attractions, was actually controlled by the Toronto Railway Company. Rides cost a dime, and there were plenty to choose from, with the favourites being "Shoot the Chute"; the gravity-defying coaster ride with the innocuous name of "Scenic Railway"; the "Cascades," a tunnel-of-love boat ride with scary interludes; and the "Airship Tour."

Shoot the Chute put riders into small, boat-shaped cars that were mechanically hauled up a long, steep incline and then let loose for a downhill scream of around eight seconds that ended with the boat car skipping and splashing into an artificial lagoon surrounded by howling spectators. Great fun, and riders not soaked by the splash down would be coaxed by cheering spectators into having another go.

The benignly named Scenic Railway was a behemoth 400-metre-long, roller-coaster-type track ride. Patrons boarded the ride cars at a depot under the athletic field grandstand and were mechanically hauled to a great height and then let go, allowing gravity to shoot the car through a series of hills and valleys into darkened tunnels.

The Cascades had riders in small boats floating through a darkened maze with monsters jumping out at almost every turn, while the Airship Tour saw patrons in miniature Zeppelins hoisted high into the air and swung about on sturdy chains.

The park offered one free ride, the Bump the Bump, and only because of the merriment it offered spectators. Participants climbed steep steps to the top of the structure, sat on their behinds on the polished wooden surface and went screaming down over various-sized mounds that threw them willy-nilly, this way and that, to end in a heap accompanied by much laughter from those on the sidelines. Other popular attractions were the funhouses: the Laugh Gallery, the House of Mirrors, the House of Nonsense and Joyland.

Disaster panoramas were popular, as were freak shows, and for a few years, patrons got to view a row of tiny, prematurely born infants being cared for in a newfangled invention called an incubator.

Lacrosse was Canada's national sport in those days, and the park featured an athletic field and its own professional team, the Torontos, who played all comers, mostly to a packed stadium of 17,000 fans. Rugby, football and baseball games would also fill the white-painted grandstand, and, in September 1909, aviator Charles Willard thrilled the crowds with the first Canadian public demonstrations of powered flight when he took off and landed on the beach several times a day.

In 1913, the TRC dumped its ownership pretensions and took over direct management of the park until 1925, when, having lost its 30-year streetcar franchise in 1921, the TRC locked the gates in an attempt to force the city to purchase the installation. However, with the city raking in big money from its Sunnyside Amusement Park leases, there was no interest in buying competition, so the TRC dismantled the great Scarboro Beach Amusement Park and sold the property to developers.

Hanlan's Point Amusement Park

During the latter part of the 19th century, summer migration to the Toronto Islands increased dramatically, with wealthy Torontonians building summer cottages, the less-affluent erecting tent cities and overnighters booking into the hotels that sprang up to cater to their needs. To provide summer residents and visitors with something to do besides wading around at the beach, the city constructed gardens and boardwalks. To keep the people coming, the Island and Dotey ferry companies put more ships into operation and constructed reception docks on the islands. To the ferry companies, the crowds they transported back and forth represented a financial opportunity, and, already experienced in providing entertainment in the form of moonlight dance cruises,

the owners put their heads together and came up with an amalgamation plan that by 1890 saw only one ferry company servicing
the waterfront, the Toronto Ferry Company (TFC).

In 1894, ostensibly to deepen the harbour for its pair of
1000-passenger ferries, the TFC dredged up more than
5 hectares of harbour bottom and dumped it at Hanlan's Point,
near to where Ned Hanlan, one of their short-term partners,
had constructed his large, gingerbread-style hotel. The TFC
created enough land to build a new destination for their ferries,
and they provided a reception dock, a baseball stadium and
a giant boardwalk on which they constructed a grand amusement park in the style of New York City's already famous Coney
Island Amusement Park.

There was something for everyone at Hanlan's Point Amusement
Park. Patrons could trip the light fantastic in its multi-tiered,
rooftop garden and dance pavilion. There were three roller coasters:
the giant "Scenic Railway," the "Switchback" and the "Circle
Eight." There was also the "Whip," an early version of the
famed Tilt-a-Whirl, a roller-skating rink, the Museum of Living
Curiosities, the Jester variety theatre, the giant slide called the
"Hurgle Gurgel" and the "Old Mill" gondola ride, affectionately
called "The Dips." There was the "Giant Swing," the "Human
Roulette Wheel," the huge "Circle Swing," a nude beach,
Hamburger's famous water show with diving horses, a huge
carousel and a baseball stadium, as well as snack concessions
and fine-dining restaurants. At night, 5000 light bulbs turned
the park into a twinkling wonderland of delights.

In 1903, disaster stuck the baseball stadium, and it burned to
the ground. In 1909, disaster struck again, and Hanlan's Hotel
burned down, along with half the amusement park and the new
baseball stadium. Rebuilt in time for the next season, the park
now featured a new roller coaster called the "Racer," a Ferris
wheel and an enlarged baseball stadium that burned to the
ground a year later. Rebuilt yet again even bigger and better,

Maple Leaf Stadium, home to the Toronto Maple Leaf professional baseball team, would see Babe Ruth smack the first fly ball of his professional career in 1914.

Hanlan's Point Amusement Park, the city's own Coney Island, packed people in night and day, and on Saturdays, the lineups at the ferry terminal looked endless. The Toronto Railway Company took a jealous gander at those long lineups and saw the same opportunity as the Toronto Ferry Company had—build a trolley park destination and the people will come. With the city already controlling a popular streetcar destination called Sunnyside Beach, all it took was a little coaxing and pointing at the ferry terminal lineups to get city councillors onside for another trolley park.

The city saw opportunity and jumped onboard by buying both Hanlan's Point Amusement Park and the TFC's ferry boats, a good deal for the TFC because, in 1926, having transferred their Maple Leaf Ball Club to a new stadium at the foot to Bathurst Street, they could see attendance falling off at the amusement park. Undaunted, but having experience building only beaches, the city wisely decided to lease out the opportunities at Sunnyside. In 1937, the city began demolition of the Hanlan's Point park to make room for the Island Airport, but parts of it—the carousel, dance hall, roller rink, several refreshment stands and a boat rental—hung on until 1955, operating as Hanlan's Memorial Park.

 One of the main attractions at Hanlan's Point Amusement Park was Hamburger's waterfront show with its famous diving horses. Nowadays, most people would classify that spectacle as being cruel to animals, but, in reality, the trained horses were never forced to jump from the 15-metre-high ramp. Diving into the water would earn the horses a bag of sugared carrots, and most were so eager to collect that they needed restraining to keep them from galloping up the ramp.

Another popular attraction at Hanlan's Point was Hamburger's exotic underwater show, which featured beautiful Maude Macdonald discarding her swimsuit in the depths of a murky pool of lake water.

DID YOU  KNOW?

The Hanlan's Point Amusement Park carousel, a 1903 product of the Charles I.D. Looff Company of Rhode Island, is alive and well and going around at Lakeside Park in Port Dalhousie near St. Catharines and Niagara Falls. The entire carousel, along with its menagerie of 69 hand-carved animals and chariots has been faithfully restored, making it a must-have experience for kids of any age.

Sunnyside Amusement Park

The area around Humber Bay is called Sunnyside and has been since John George Howard, owner of the expansive property called High Park, erected a summer home that he called Sunnyside on a promontory overlooking the bay. In 1873, Howard deeded his house, Colborne Lodge, and his estate to the people of Toronto. During the 1880s, the city installed a water-pumping station at

Sunnyside that somehow altered the lake current and created a fine beach that attracted swimmers. To make visits to Sunnyside Beach more enjoyable, the city constructed a boardwalk along the beach for the weekend enjoyment of people wanting sunshine or a swim in the clear water. *A nice spot for a cottage*, thought visitors, and with the city amenable to granting leases, cottages sprouted up like mushrooms.

In 1892, the Toronto Railway and Electric Company's electric streetcars began running to Sunnyside, attracting more people to come for a turn on the boardwalk. Taken over the following year by the Toronto Railway Company, the streetcars became double-deckers, allowing for more weekenders. At the turn of the century, sensing financial opportunity, Mrs. Pauline Meyer opened a large restaurant on Sunnyside's boardwalk, serving her specialty fresh fish dinners.

Sunnyside was booming, but, in 1912, the city dismantled the pumping station and the beach began to erode. Concerned cottagers and locals appealed to the Toronto Harbour Commission to fix the problem, and they responded by awarding a local resident, Mr. Emil Brooker, the right to build a bathhouse on the beach and charge admission. Then, after realizing that not everyone could afford or wanted to pay for a swim, the Harbour Commission constructed a free beach just west of the Brooker establishment that included a tame version of the Scarboro Beach Amusement Park's Shoot the Chute water slide.

In 1913, the Harbour Commission included Sunnyside in its massive plan to deepen Toronto Harbour and upgrade the entire waterfront, a project that would see 300,000 cubic metres of sandy muck dredged from the harbour and distributed along a 6-kilometre stretch of western waterfront. Work began in 1913, and, by 1917, Sunnyside had a fine beach and the Pavilion Restaurant and dance hall with a décor and first-class dinning service that wowed patrons.

By 1921, now calling itself Toronto's Lakeside Playground, Sunnyside had a paved Boulevard Road, now called Lakeshore Boulevard West, a new boardwalk promenade and beach, a newly constructed bathing pavilion, the Palais Royale dance hall (originally a boat rental location) and room for some thrills and frills. From hundreds of applications, the Harbour Commission picked seven rides, with six to be operated by the Sunnyside Amusement Company: three swing rides, two Coney Island sensations, the spinning, tilting "Frolic," the smash up "Dodgem" and a large, delightful carousel. One ride licence, for the complicated and thrilling Coney Island "Whip," went to J.B. Atkinson, an American with experience operating that ride. Nine games of skill, to be operated by one J.R. McIntyre, along with 10 refreshment stand licences would complete the nucleus of an amusement park, and on Wednesday, June 28, 1922, Sunnyside Beach Amusement Park opened its gates to massive crowds. The crowds just kept coming, and the mostly staid rides that opened the park were soon replaced by larger, more thrilling devices such as the "Flyer" roller coaster and the Coney Island–style steeplechase ride, the "Derby Racer."

The park got a baseball diamond in 1924 and promoted women's baseball, and, in 1927, construction began on Sunnyside's principle attraction, the Palace Pier, with its huge dance pavilion. Meant to emulate the famous Palace Pier in Brighton Beach, England, the endeavour met with all kinds of problems and was not completed until 1941, but this was still in time to host almost all of the era's big bands at its humungous dance hall. Beginning in 1929, nighttime attendance was promoted through the torching of old sailing ships. In 1936, Sunnyside got Honeydew, its signature orange drink, which was usually accompanied by the wonderful steamed hot dog called Red Hot and the buttery-soft, legendary Downyflake doughnut.

An easy 30 minutes from the city by streetcar from almost anywhere in the city, Sunnyside could be reached even more quickly by automobile, a mode of transportation that would cause the demise of both Hanlan's Point and the mighty Scarboro Beach Amusement Park, and eventually Sunnyside itself. After the wartime rationing of tires and gasoline ended, people took to the roads and forgot about the thrills and frills at Sunnyside and, as early as 1948, city officials were talking of tearing it down and building a throughway. Sunnyside hung on, with concessionaires operating on yearly leases, but at its end in 1955, Toronto's grandest entertainment venue looked tired and ready for the wrecker's ball. Today, all that remains of Sunnyside Amusement Park is the renovated Palais Royale dance hall and the Art Deco bathing pavilion in a city area still called Sunnyside.

At midnight on July 19, 1929, an airplane swooped from the night sky above Sunnyside Amusement Park and firebombed the venerable old ferry boat *Ned Hanlan*. Billed by park manager Lawrence "Sol" Solmon as "a midnight roman candle celebration" the burning created an attendance boon for the park that sent Sol scrambling to acquire more old ships to light up the night sky at Sunnyside.

PARK SNACK ICONS

Honey Dew

Before there was Honey Dew, the orange-drink favourite of generations of Torontonians, there was Flora-Dew, dispensed by the Ryan brothers from their food concession at Hanlan's Point Amusement Park. Honey Dew was a "secret formula" creation of the Lindsays, four brothers from Aylmer, who, in 1921, began bottling Orange Crush in St. Thomas under licence from Crush inventor Clayton J. Howell of Los Angeles. Business boomed, and, in 1922, they moved the operation to Toronto.

In 1925, looking for new ways to distribute Orange Crush, they acquired a small restaurant chain called Honey Dew, whose orange drink and hot dog format copied that of the Ryan brothers' Hanlan's Point Flora-Dew food concession. However, this company's orange drink product was not up to the brothers' standards, so using expertise garnered through the mixing of Orange Crush syrup, they devised a new and secret formulation for Honey Dew.

The new drink was much appreciated by Torontonians, but Honey Dew remained a local favourite, while the brother's Orange Crush business soared across the nation, enabling the Lindsays to list shares on the Toronto Stock Exchange. All was well until the stock market collapsed in the early 1930s, giving beer tycoon Edward "E.P." Taylor the opportunity to pick up the shares for peanuts. Taylor wanted the Crush bottling business, not the Honey Dew restaurants, but over the next few years, that changed, and as one of only three people privy to the drink's secret formulation, he would personally attend the once-a-month, locked-door mixing of the secret ingredients that went into the Honey Dew drink base.

Backed by E.P. Taylor's millions, Honey Dew became ubiquitous in Toronto, with a restaurant on almost every street, several stands at both the CNE and Sunnyside Amusement Park, and even a stand at the Simpson's store. In the early 1950s, Taylor sold the Honey Dew Company to J. William Horsey's Salada Foods, and the orange drink and Red Hot hot dog, food items synonymous with a good time in Toronto, gradually retreated from city streets to Sunnyside Amusement Park and the CNE. Today, the orange-drink favourite of generations of Torontonians is available in the frozen section of some supermarkets and at the CNE, albeit with a slight change to the secret formula, which I do believe was orange oil along with a good splash of methyl bromide to maintain suspension.

Red Hot

The obligatory steamed hot dog that accompanied a Flora-Dew, the famous Red Hot, was an 1880 invention of Baltimore street sausage vendor Antonoine Feuchtwanger, or more precisely his wife, who thought customers would appreciate a long, steam-softened bun to prevent mustard-stained hands. He called his sausages in long, steamed buns Red Hots.

However, the institutionalizing of hot dogs at amusement parks is attributed to Coney Island pie-cart vendor Charlie Feltman's 1867 decision to add a sandwich to the fare offered on his travel-ling pie wagon. Having no space on his cart to make a sandwich, Charlie devised a metal cabinet to keep buns fresh and a charcoal heater to boil water to cook sausages and fitted them onto his cart. Charlie's ready-made sausage sandwiches earned him money enough to branch into beer gardens, food stands and rides to amuse his customers.

The hot dog remained just a sausage on a bun, or what Adolph Gehring was calling them while hawking sausages to the crowds at the St. Louis baseball stadium, "Meat sandwiches, get your red hot meat sandwiches," until a customer yelled, "Gimme one of them hot...dogs." Other customers began demanding "hot dogs," and the iconic name was born. However, the real hero of hot dogs was a fellow named Nathan Handwerker, an employee of Charlie Feltman, who, in 1906, set up his own Coney Island hot dog stand at the corner of Surf and Stillwell Avenues, calling it Nathan's.

Toronto Showbiz

Tons of movies are shot in Toronto,
but Toronto is never Toronto.

—Eugene Levy, comedian

OVERTURE, CURTAIN, LIGHTS

During the city's formative years, Toronto's citizenry, both rural and urban, found entertainment through the presentation of food. Country folk had their Sunday suppers, barn raisings and harvest festivals, and townspeople had their grand dinner parties. Although the rural affairs were entertaining, they were generally of short duration (the participants were early risers), with the menu limited to game, chicken and things from the garden or root cellar.

Downtown was a different kettle of fish; urbanites' dinner parties would begin in the late afternoon, feature five or six courses with dozens of wines and liquors, and run far into the evening. These were competitive dinners, with host and hostess vying for the best table of the year with social or career advancement being the blue ribbon. Nowadays, one can hardly fathom the button-busting scope of those dinners: 18 guests, five or six roasts with their gravies, three kinds of fish, every vegetable in season and condiments galore, all interspersed with speeches and countless toasts with the finest claret. Afterward came sherry or port with more toasting and four or five desert choices, which ended with the men waddling off for cigars and brandy into one room, while the women retired to another to talk about what they missed most about Britain…fancy-dress balls and the theatre.

Touring Troupe Theatres

By 1809, ladies not on the highest rungs of York's social ladder stopped talking about theatre and tripped out to see the occasional American touring troupe perform at a local tavern. Then, around 1820, the city got a kind of theatre district when the Colborne Street Theatre opened and the nearby Frank's Hotel began hosting touring troupes in their second-floor ballroom. In 1925, Frank's even staged an opera performance to rave reviews. During the 1830s, touring troupe theatres sprang up like mushrooms, with Keating's Coffee House deemed appropriate for even the highest members of Toronto society.

The city reached a social milestone in 1846 when it got a new city hall with a ballroom upstairs, as well as the almost-1200-seat Lyceum Theatre, which opened in a vacant building on King Street near to where the Royal Alex stands today. The Lyceum proved so successful that it prompted construction of the 740-seat Royal Lyceum Theatre on the south side of King between York and Bay Streets. The Royal Lyceum was Toronto's first purpose-built theatre, and audiences packed the house almost every night. The city's social scene had switched from belly-buster dinners to theatre, but its upper rung wanted more of what Frank's Hotel had staged in the early 1820s…opera.

The Opera Houses

From 1850 to 1875, Toronto got no less than six opera houses, culminating in the opulent, 1200-seat Grand Opera House on Adelaide Street. The upper crust of Toronto society was set for their nights on the town, but common folk needed entertainment, too, and to fill that need, the newly constructed railways brought touring groups of comedians, jugglers, wirewalkers, singers and dog acts. This was a something-for-everybody form of entertainment—a variety of acts born out of the rural travelling medicine shows and brought to the masses sans alcohol. This form of clean, family-style entertainment proved so popular that performance troupes were held over for long-term engagements, and that required either the construction of new venues or, in the case of Toronto, a takeover of some of the city's opera houses. Europeans called this new form of family-style entertainment "variety," while in the U.S. and Canada, it was called "vaudeville."

From the time the theatre opened in 1884 until 1888, the manager of the ultra-deluxe Toronto Opera House was a woman, famed actress Charlotte Morris—an unusual occurrence for a time when a woman's place was in the home, period.

The Scottish Play

On November 28, 1879, the Grand Opera House, at 9-15 Adelaide Street West, caught fire and burned immediately after a production of Shakespeare's play *Macbeth*, adding credence to the play's reputation for being an unlucky production.

DID YOU  KNOW?

Electric arc lighting was still a novelty when Toronto's Grand Opera House opened on September 23, 1874, and to capitalize on the public's interest, the Opera House featured the "Elegant Prismatic Reflecting Sunlight Chandelier." Illuminated by an arc lamp, the giant chandelier was turned on nightly at 7:45 PM to dazzle patrons until the curtain was raised.

Vaudeville

No one is sure where the word "vaudeville" originated, but most historians attribute its common usage in the U.S. and Canada to New York impresario Tony Pastor, a former circus ringmaster turned theatre owner. In 1881, Pastor took the best from all forms of variety entertainment, cleaned up the acts, got rid of alcohol and undesirable elements, and featured what he called "vaudeville entertainment" on the stage of his uptown theatres. It was clean family entertainment for the masses, and the venues soon became huge and extremely profitable. From about 1885 to the late 1920s, vaudeville was a phenomenal hit in Toronto, and while many theatres were constructed for that purpose, none had more pizzazz than Shea's 2000-seat Victory Theatre on the southeast corner of Richmond and Victoria Streets. The Victory had interior decorations that rivalled those of European opera houses, and for a short time, it was North America's largest and finest vaudeville theatre, an iconic precursor to future monumental motion picture venues as film gradually pushed out the variety acts.

The Shea brothers then constructed another spectacular vaude-ville venue, the Yonge Street Theatre, but it was their third act that wowed the populace, their fabulous Hippodrome, also known as the Hip. Constructed north of Queen on Terauley Street, now Bay Street, the Hip was a theatre like no other. It sat 3200 people under a huge, illuminated, glass dome, dripped gilded plaster deco-rations like an Italian opera house and featured an orchestra pit, 12 opera boxes and innovative lighting. Considered one of the greatest vaudeville venues in North America, Shea's Hippodrome attracted the finest talent, stars such as Eddie Cantor, Buster Keaton, Will Rogers, George Burns and Gracie Allen, and Toronto's own O'Connor Sisters, at the time considered the finest singing group of the vaudeville era.

With the coming of motion pictures, the popularity of vaudeville declined rapidly. The death knell for Toronto vaudeville occurred on the cold, blustery midnight of December 28, 1928, when Warner Brothers' second talkie production, *The Terror,* opened at the Allan's Tivoli theatre on Victoria Street to a sold-out house of 1500.

The Panoramas

Beginning around 1860, the ubiquitous travelling medicine shows wandering North America's towns and countryside began catering to the public's craving for world news by painting pictorial displays onto sheets of canvas and hanging them on the sides of barns and buildings. They were called "panoramas," and they became very popular, especially in larger towns and cities with a more cosmopolitan population interested in foreign affairs.

By 1887, Toronto had indeed become cosmopolitan, and sensing financial opportunity, the Toronto Cyclorama Company constructed a massive, 16-sided, domed building on Front Street for the visual entertainment of residents. Paintings of historical or current events, called "cycloramas," hung from the 16 sides of the building and provided spectators with a 360-degree visual experience that knocked their socks off. Unfortunately for the Cyclorama people, that experience was too soon being enjoyed in homes, because, in 1888, the Underwood & Underwood Company, manufacturers of stereoscopes and stereoscopic slides, established a branch in the city and their agents began hawking instruments and slides from door to door.

The slides and viewers proved highly successful, especially Underwood's stereoscope 3D slides featuring world events, as Toronto's citizenry were hungry for world news. The most popular slides dealt with the European war between the French and Prussian alliance, for which Underwood had dispatched photographers to cover the battles. For a population accustomed to viewing the world through dated lithographs in books,

Underwood's up-to-date, ultra-realistic 3D pictures were a technological wake-up call. The city's entrepreneurs immediately began looking for some way to commercialize the company's home sensation.

DID YOU KNOW?

In 1898, the city took over the dome-topped Cyclorama building for non-payment of taxes and used it as a warehouse and, later, a parking garage. Many city residents may still remember the curious-looking structure because it wasn't demolished until 1972.

Peep Shows

Beginning around 1890, the Mutoscope, or peep show—where the customer looks into a box and winds through a series of sequential cards—became popular at fairs, circuses and exhibitions, but though it hinted at technological advance, it was a simple curiosity. Nevertheless, the inquisitive had money and wanted desperately to wind thrills a minute from a machine that provided only 30 seconds of moving pictures. To help them out, peep show impresarios rented storefronts and installed banks of Mutoscopes that enabled thrill seekers to wind through an entire row loaded with different cards. Everybody loved the peep shows, and the curiosity aroused the interest of American inventor Thomas Edison. On May 20, 1891, Edison demonstrated a motorized peep show with a three-second film in place of cards at a meeting of the National Federation of Women's Clubs in New York City. The inventor called his improved peep show a Kinetoscope and entrusted its distribution to the Holland brothers, two boys from Ottawa trying for the big time in New York City and later Toronto.

The Dime Museums

The price of admission was a dime—hence the name—and once inside, customers sat and watched jugglers, acrobats and tight-rope walkers strut their stuff. Every city had a least three or four of these variety theatres in rented buildings and storefronts, and the theatres usually included an adjunct museum of oddities where spectators could walk about and get their thrills viewing two-headed calves in formaldehyde, shrunken heads, Egyptian mummies and the like. Among the oddities, dime museum pro-prietors would install a bank of Mutoscopes, most containing an added thrill through risqué cards. Toronto had many dime museums with peepshows, but, in 1894, after Thomas Edison demonstrated the Kinetoscope at the CNE, the new device quickly pushed the Mutoscopes out and became the big money-maker for dime museums. Meanwhile, back in the U.S., old Tom Edison got hold of an improved version of his Kinetoscope, one that projected images out from the box onto a white sheet—the Vitascope. Not his invention, but he made a number of improvements to the machine and marketed it as his own.

In 1886, Torontonians saw their first projected motion pictures when Robinson's Musee Theatre, a dime museum at Robinson and Richmond Streets, installed a Vitascope machine in its main-floor variety theatre. On a curious coincidental note, one of Robinson's opening films, a hand-coloured rendition of La Loie Fuller doing her famous "Butterfly Dance," could also be viewed live at the Toronto Opera House as the famous danseuse was making her one and only Canadian appearance. Another odd coincidence is that just a few minutes after Robinson started up his Vitascope machine for the first time, right across the street, the Lumiere Cinematographe cranked up its own competitive moving-picture machine.

That same year, Edison perfected his own version of the Vitascope and, calling it the Projecting Kinetoscope, began to market the machine along with short films produced in-house. Storefront motion picture parlours sprang up throughout Toronto, with hordes of people paying a nickel to view 90 seconds of moving pictures on a bedsheet.

In the U.S., they called the parlours "nickelodeons," as did Torontonians until 1906, when John C. Griffin opened the city's first large-venue movie theatre, calling it "the Theatorium," a name synonymous with movie houses to Torontonians for generations. Part movie, part vaudeville theatre, the Theatorium was Griffin's second movie house in a venture that would see him open a dozen more across Ontario .

THE GRAND MOVIE PALACES

The Ouimetoscope

Montréal electrical engineer Léo-Ernest Ouimet had a thing for lighting. In 1901, when he was only 24 years old, he rewired and installed innovative lighting in two of that city's legitimate theatres. In 1902, Léo attended a Sunday night variety show at the city's 5000-seat, open-air pavilion in Sohmers Park, where he witnessed an intermission demonstration of Edison's new Projecting Kinetoscope. Intrigued, he contacted Edison and, in 1903, he received a distributorship for eastern Canada.

Léo was happy with the arrangement but not with Edison's projector, and, by 1904, he had fiddled the machine into projecting larger images and in a way that stopped the annoying flicker. Léo called his improved projector the Ouimetoscope, and he took it on the road, doing outdoor shows in poorer neighbourhoods. These were large, well-attended affairs, and they provided Léo with an idea—his Ouimetoscope could project larger images inside as well as out, so why not show big pictures inside?

Léo purchased an abandoned cabaret on Montréal's St. Catherine Street, gussied it up with red and gold paint and installed some interesting lighting and 500 comfortable chairs. The theatre was such a hit that after a few years, Léo tore it down and built another with 1200 seats, calling it the Ouimetoscope. Léo put all the gold plaster and balconies found in ritzy, legitimate theatres into his cathedral-sized movie house along with something new—air conditioning. Léo opened his Ouimetoscope on August 31, 1907, to a packed house and sold out every seat for years. Future movie moguls came to Montréal from Toronto and around the world to see Léo's fantastic theatre, and they would use his ideas in building their own grand movie palaces.

The Pantages (Imperial) Theatre War

In 1920, Nathan L. Nathanson, a former Scarboro Beach Amusement Park concessionaire and founder of the Famous Players Theatre chain (the Canadian division of movie mogul Adolph Zukor's Paramount Pictures) opened the largest, most elaborate movie house in North America, the 3337-seat Pantages Theatre. Although Nathanson owned the Pantages, Alexander Pantages handled the management and film bookings, and all theatres in his circuit of 120 movie houses were called Pantages. In both Canada and the U.S., the Pantages circuit monopolized theatre on the west coast, while the Keith-Albee-Orpheum Circuit, or KAO, held sway in the east.

In 1928, bootlegger and politico Joe Kennedy and David Sarnoff, principle shareholder of RCA, acquired control of KAO, changed the name to Radio Keith Orpheum (RKO) and made Pantages an offer for his theatre chain. Pantages refused, but the next year, he was arrested and tried for the rape of a 17-year-old chorus girl, a charge eventually proved to be spurious and perhaps engineered by Kennedy and Sarnoff. Businessmen played hardball in those days, and that game broke Alexander Pantages financially, forcing him to sell out to RKO for much less than the original offer. Owner Nathanson took the Pantages name down from his Yonge Street theatre marquee and put up a new name—Imperial Theatre.

In 1972, Famous Players closed the Imperial Theatre after a first-run showing of the *Godfather* for a 10-month redesign by Toronto architect Mandel Sprachman into six smaller cinemas with a name change to the Imperial Six Theatre. During this reconstruction, a few friends and I would take lunchtime tours of this grand facility courtesy of a backdoor key provided by Nat Nathanson's son Paul during one of my personal-memo deliveries to him from the London-based Rank Organization, the founder of the Odeon Theatre chain through which my old boss, Oscar Hanson, had a film distributorship. Paul controlled a lot of theatre stock, and while I never read any of the memos, I can imagine that they were concerned with ongoing manoeuvrings by various companies to acquire that stock as Viacom did in 1994 with their acquisition of Famous Players stock.

And the war? It began back in 1920 when Nat Nathanson built the Pantages Theatre. Nat was unable to buy all the land on which to build his fabulous theatre; he could buy only the southern half of the property, and he leased the northern half from a family in Michigan. Over the years, this division of property presented no problems—until 1986, when Famous Players Realty, the New York–based real estate arm of Famous Players, tried to renew the lease with a lowball, take-it-or-leave-it offer. They told the Michigan owner of the property, a little old lady, that no one else would be interested in leasing half a movie theatre. Big mistake, because back in Toronto, a rival theatre company called Cineplex Odeon, the precursor to Viacom, was indeed interested, and CEO Garth Drabinsky made a mad dash to Michigan to sign a lease. The next day, Drabinsky had his newly acquired northern section of the Imperial 6 Theatre sectioned off with wallboard, effectively blocking Famous Players from the building.

Drabinsky divided his half of the building into three theatres with an entrance on Victoria Street. One day before Cineplex's grand opening, Famous Players called upon the fire department to check on Cineplex's newly constructed fire exits. The exits were found to be deficient, and the grand opening was switched to another Cineplex venue, the Varsity Cinema, with the Cineplex opening rescheduled for the next day.

Famous Players scuttled that opening as well by removing all the doors from their exits, allowing winter air into the entire building and freezing out moviegoers. Cineplex's response was to sabotage Famous Players' popcorn delivery, and the conflict went back and forth until finally, in 1988, Famous Players threw in the towel and sold their half of the theatre to Cineplex in a deal that required Cineplex to never show movies in that section.

CEO Garth Drabinsky had always wanted to be involved with legitimate theatre, and that time had arrived.

After extensive renovations, the "new" 2200-seat Pantages Theatre opened to rave reviews. However, the war would continue, with various corporate media giants vying for control of Cineplex, a wrestling match that finally ended in 2008, when England's huge Key Brand Entertainment Company bought Cineplex and sold the Pantages Imperial to Toronto theatre impresario Ed Mirvish and it became his Canon Theatre.

THEATRE FOLK

Our Mary

In 1898, Toronto's own Gladys Smith made her first stage appearance at the Princess Theatre in a play called *The Silver King*. She was five years old and spoke only one line. Gladys Smith would later change her name to Mary Pickford and become a Hollywood legend.

Red Gets Famous

In 1936, Red Skelton, a then unknown comedian, appeared onstage at Shea's Hippodrome and left one year later, having become a star.

What ever happened to Ambrose Small? That question has confounded historians and police ever since he disappeared on December 2, 1919. Although many Torontonians have disappeared over the years, and a few have attracted the public's attention, none has created more interest then the disappearance of Grand Opera House owner Ambrose Small. The cause of the singular interest is the $1.7 million he deposited in his bank account some hours before he vanished, a cheque he had received from the sale of a his chain of theatres in seven Canadian cities.

After depositing the money, Ambrose Small had lunch with his wife, Theresa, and returned to his office at the Grand Opera House. Later that afternoon, he left the opera house, bought a newspaper and walked off into what was, according to a 1936 report by an OPP inspector named Edward Hammond, a murder trap sprung by his wife and his personal secretary, John Doughty.

Inspector Hammond claimed that the case was a cover-up by Toronto police because of Theresa Small's social prominence, but because he didn't file his report until a year after her death, his report was and still is regarded as supposition. No trace of Ambrose Small has ever been found, and the mystery continues, but not for the Toronto police, as they grew tired of answering questions about the case from amateur sleuths and reporters, and they destroyed the file in 1960.

The Lost Seat

During restoration of the Elgin and Winter Garden theatres during the 1980s, restoration staff found that some seats had gone missing, so they contacted the Biograph Theatre in Chicago, a restored venue with seating manufactured by the same company.

The Biograph had installed new seating during restoration and helpfully sent over a few dozen old seats from storage, one of which was an odd colour. Not until after that odd seat had been recovered and installed who knows where in the theatre did any-one inquire why that one seat was different. As it turns out, it was the seat occupied by famed bank robber John Dillinger before he was gunned down by FBI agents while leaving the theatre, so somewhere in the Elgin Theatre is an icon to John Dillinger's "last picture show."

The Wars

*Have you ever seen the United States take the blame
for anything?*

–former mayor Mel Lastman

A CHILD OF WAR

The Good from the Bad

Toronto owes its very existence to war; if not for the threat from U.S. cannons, Niagara-on-the-Lake might have been Ontario's capital city. The threat of invasion prompted the formation of the city's street system, the placement of government buildings and the general structure of the harbour. The early European wars required massive amounts of lumber to build ships, grain to feed troops and a destination to send displaced populations—and Toronto was that place.

The U.S. Civil War and later European wars inundated the waterfront with all manner of industries to supply the necessities of battle. War trimmed the city's male population, moved women out of the home into wartime industries and got them the vote, while those industries contributed vast amounts of pollution that gave rise to more sewer construction and a cleaner water supply. Old wars ran on whisky, which the city produced in such huge quantities that for most of the 19th century, it was the world's largest supplier. Military conflicts required guns, ammunition and medicines, and the city's new industrial might was ready to supply it all.

Toronto was born, shaped, enriched and made to suffer by wars. Torontonians have fought in many wars under many flags, with those that had the most effect on the city being the Stars and Stripes, the British Union Jack and, finally, our own flag.

THE U.S. CIVIL WAR

The Underground Railway

In spite of Canada's historical connection with the American abolitionist movement and its famous Underground Railway, many Torontonians were sympathetic to the Confederacy, a fact that very nearly derailed Canadian sovereignty.

The bombardment of Fort Sumter in Charleston Harbour by Confederate forces on April 12, 1861, signalled the start of one of the bloodiest conflicts in the annals of warfare. In Toronto, news of the attack caused an immediate polarizing of society, with slavery abolitionists siding with the North and those with anti-American sentiments supporting the South. Back in 1850, the U.S. Congress had amended the Fugitive Slave Act of 1793 making it a federal crime to harbour slaves in any state of the Union, thus making Canada, especially Ontario, an extension of the "underground railway" and the final destination for thousands of freed slaves. Their safety depended on a line on a map, a border constantly ignored by U.S. marshals and men hunting runaways for bounty money. These border incursions infuriated Ontarians, and their outrage was exacerbated by the kidnapping of runaways from Toronto, whose citizens blamed the U.S government and their suspected aspirations to annex Canada into the Union.

A Threat from Across the Border

In Toronto, no one thought the war would last more than a few months, especially after news of the Union's defeat at the Battle of Bull Run reached the city. However, go on it did, degenerating into a slugfest that quickly depleted supplies of ordnance, food and men on both sides, a situation that proved financially beneficial for Canada. Union naval forces had blockaded Southern ports, but they couldn't stop Canada's maritime ship captains from routinely running supplies to the Confederacy. In Québec, ships crossed the St. Lawrence River in a solid mass, and the newly constructed Victoria Bridge at Montréal was jammed with trains heading for New York. In Ontario, border crossings plugged solid with wagons carrying supplies to Union forces made Lake Erie crossings popular.

The war was a financial boon for Canada West but was thought to be politically dangerous because a victorious Union might decide to send forces north into Canada, an idea that was being bandied about in the U.S. Congress. Torontonians were especially fearful because, in 1859, rabid abolitionist John Brown had used the Chatham area as a base from which to launch an attack on the U.S. armoury at Harpers Ferry, and a reprisal was fully expected. A city already suspicious of U.S. intentions was fertile ground for Confederate spies and agitators, especially after the 1861 Trent Affair, in which two diplomats accredited by the Confederacy were seized on November 8 from a Union-intercepted British mail packet called the *Trent*. This contravention of maritime law pushed Britain to the brink of war with the U.S., an action only narrowly averted when the U.S. released the envoys and apologized to Britain for their detainment.

However, British troops had already flooded into Upper Canada, putting Toronto on a virtual war footing with the U.S. This situation would help spur Canada to Confederation in 1867 to better deal with a feared invasion. Military incursions by disbanded northern forces united by the Fenian Brotherhood did occur in 1866–67, after the war had ended, and though they were easily repulsed, those attacks had a hurrying up effect on Confederation. The Trent Affair proved enormously lucky for Toronto because on May 31, 1866, a force of almost a thousand Fenians crossed the border at Niagara Falls, intending to move down the Niagara Peninsula to Toronto only to be stopped by a militia created during the Trent Affair's escalation of tension between the U.S. and Canada.

Another bit of luck for the city was the defeat of General George Armstrong Custer's 7th Cavalry at Little Big Horn in 1876 because it caused the government to divert U.S. troops from a railway construction project into Manitoba to chase Chief Sitting Bull. Without Manitoba, there would have been no transcontinental railway and no wheat shipments for Toronto's burgeoning harbour traffic.

Canadians in the American Civil War

There were approximately 20,000 Canadian volunteers serving on either side in the Civil War. Many failed to return or returned disabled, and many were Torontonians.

Why did they join? Some were abolitionists, some were "crimped" or press-ganged and some went for adventure, but most went in the last years of the war for the bounty paid to volunteers by the North in a desperate effort to expand its army. Each volunteer private was paid $300, an annual wage for many of Toronto's younger citizens, while the bounty paid to officers could be as high as $1250 along with a 160-acre (65-hectare) land grant.

The Northwest Conspiracy

In February 1864, a desperate Confederate Congress authorized the expenditure of $5 million in gold for the sabotage of enemy property on land or sea. Of that expenditure, $1 million went to support the Canadian operations of Confederate Captain Thomas Hines headquartered at the Queen's Hotel in Toronto.

Hines was in the city to foment insurrection in the U.S. Northwest, an area now called the American Midwest, and he used the Grand Trunk Railway (GTR) to enter the U.S. via Windsor for the recruitment of Southern sympathizers in Ohio, Indiana and Illinois. By all accounts, he was very good at his job, forcing the Union to divert forces from the frontlines into these areas to counter the activities of subversive groups called "copperheads," so named because they used the head of President Lincoln cut from a penny as an ironic form of identification.

Although Hines was brilliant, there was a flaw in his organization—his communication with the Confederate Secret Service depended on couriers, and one of those messengers was a double agent. So when Hines hit upon a plan to free thousands of POWs from Johnson's Island—a Union prison camp on an island in Lake Erie off Sandusky, Ohio—Union authorities in Washington knew all about it and successfully foiled the attempt. Undaunted, Hines would make a second attempt at freeing POWs, this time from the camp at Fort Douglas in Chicago, Illinois. That effort was thwarted by the fort's commanding officer, who was alerted that Chicago was filling up with copperheads and Canadian Confederate sympathizers and struck first, arresting most of the conspirators and seizing their arms cache.

Hines would try many tricks of sabotage including an attempt to burn down hotels in New York City using time bombs, most of which failed to detonate. His other acts of subversion included the successful St. Albans bank raid and the distribution of contaminated clothing and blankets collected by a doctor while treating yellow fever victims in Bermuda. While the bank raid added considerably to Hines' sabotage fund, the diseased rags were a bust as no outbreaks were reported.

Although there is no corroborating evidence, Hines may have been the instigator of a plot to kidnap President Lincoln that went terribly wrong, ending with the president's assassination. Evidence exists that indicates Lincoln's killer, actor John Wilkes Booth, was in Canada just prior to the assassination, while just after, Hines was in Detroit, where he created a red-herring impersonation of Booth that caused Union pursuers to believe Booth had escaped to Canada.

After Lee's surrender at Appomattox, Hines used his spy fund and contacts to help Confederate luminaries escape Union retribution by absconding to Canada. Hines stayed in Toronto studying law with fellow exile Confederate General John C. Breckinridge until the U.S. granted amnesty in 1866, when he returned home to Kentucky to become a lawyer and eventually serve as Chief Justice of the Kentucky Court of Appeal.

A Prime Sympathizer

Years before the onset of the Civil War, many Southern families had summer homes in the Niagara Falls area, and Torontonians were familiar with Southern gentility and much preferred those folks to the coarse Northerners.

George Denison, scion of a wealthy and prominent Toronto family, at only 22 years of age, commanded the 1st Volunteer Cavalry city militia unit and was a staunch supporter of the Southern cause. Denison, who had many Southern friends, had visited General Robert E. Lee in Richmond and harboured Confederate agents at his home during the war's entirety.

Coins of Our Own

Toronto's economy boomed during the American Civil War years, and as neither Union nor Confederate banknotes were trusted as payment for goods or services, the city—along with the entire country—became inundated with U.S. gold coinage. Leery of monetary assimilation by the U.S., the Canadian government immediately arranged with Britain for the minting of both gold and silver Canadian coins.

THE BOER WAR

Torontonians in South Africa

Of the more than 8600 soldiers and 12 female nurses sent from Canada to South Africa to aid the British in their war against the Orange Free State and the Transvaal Republic, around 2500 hailed from Toronto. At the outbreak of hostilities on October 11, 1899, Canada immediately offered Britain troops, but Lord Carnarvon, the British Secretary of War, suggested that they send only a token force because the British foresaw no difficulty in defeating an army of untrained Afrikaners of Dutch descent, called the Boers.

Time has a way of erasing bad memories, and for the British army in South Africa, that memory was a previous battle with the Boers, a brief but bloody conflict in which the British took a beating from those untrained farmers, with the bloodiest encounter occurring at the Battle of Majuba Hill on February 27, 1881. "Remember Majuba" would be a British rallying cry for the far greater Second Boer War that began on October 11, 1899, and ended on May 31, 1902.

Canada raised its initial token force of 1000 volunteers from across the nation—mostly farm boys looking for adventure, but the group would include 39 members from the Queen's Own Rifles in Toronto, along with almost 100 volunteers from both the city and nearby communities such as Hamilton. The war would be a one-way trip for many. The British army fared badly, and Britain suggested that Canada send more volunteers. Six more units were dispatched along with officers possessed of clearer heads than their British counterparts.

By the war's end, Canada had lost 277 men, a small number compared to the 5774 British soldiers killed, but still a costly lesson for Toronto adventure seekers. Sadly, during the final year of the

Boer War, almost 50,000 Boers would die in British-invented "concentration camps," including 20,000 women and children. Another sad occurrence of the Boer War was the million or so horses killed during the conflict. The war was a fiasco, and Canadian soldiers who had volunteered to fight for one year wanted out. In spite of pleading by British generals to stay, they wisely insisted on repatriation.

A map of the Transvaal's major gold and diamond deposits correspondents so closely with a map of Boer War battle sites that the object of the conflict was unmistakable; the British wanted the gold and diamonds, and their soldiers were expendable.

DID YOU KNOW?

Censored information fed to the media on the Boer War, including news briefs made available to Toronto newspapers, contained falsehoods and disinformation prepared by author Sir Arthur Conan Doyle of Sherlock Holmes fame.

A Helping Hand

During the war, Toronto's citizens contributed over $3 million to aid, supply comfort and equip troops with extra weaponry and insurance. Money-raising initiatives abounded in Toronto; women's groups sold baked and knitted goods, children scoured neighbourhoods for paper and metals, and workers subscribed a portion of their wages to help the Canadian Patriotic Fund.

The Boy Soldiers

Young Douglas Williams of Toronto yearned for adventure and found it as a bugler with the city's Queen's Own Rifles as part of the first Canadian contingent to take part in the Boer War. At the Battle of Sunnyside, he carried dispatches and earned praise from his officers. Later, at the Battle of Paardeberg,

Williams ignored flying bullets and blew the signal to charge on his bugle while standing atop an anthill, a brave action that precipitated one of the worst disasters of the war, with 21 Canadians killed.

Young Williams (he lied about his age, but was probably 15) got his picture in every newspaper and became something of a hero to Canadians at home. Accompanying Williams was an even younger bugler, Edwin McCormick, who, at only 14 years of age, enlisted as a bugler in famous RCMP-turned-soldier Sam Steele's Lord Strathcona's Horse, also part of Canada's first Boer War contingent. Young McCormick's heroic action in various battles made him a stellar figure to the folks back home.

Both Williams and McCormick survived and returned to Canada with their regiments to volunteer again with the fourth contingent. Both boys blew their bugles at battles, burials and boondoggles and became even more famous, and, happily, both survived the war and returned to Toronto, where they received a hero's welcome.

WORLD WAR I

To War

From 1914 to 1918, Toronto sent 70,000 officers and men into
World War I with less than half returning unscathed: 13,000
were killed, 20,000 were seriously wounded and 10,000 suffered
psychological damage. It was an unmitigated disaster for both
the city and the entire country as it polarized political thinking
for generations. French Canada wanted no part of the "English
war" but, in 1917, Prime Minister Borden's government imposed
a conscription act, and French Canadians either served or
went to jail, a situation that further isolated Québec from the
Canadian political mainstream. Being mostly of British descent,
Torontonians served willingly, both "over there" and on the

home front. The war changed the city; women moved from the home into the workplace and got the vote, censorship was rampant and the investigation and internment of citizens of suspect loyalties became commonplace.

In the second week of April 1917, word reached the city of Canada's fantastic victory at Vimy Ridge, and the city turned out to celebrate. However, that celebratory mood turned to mourning a few months later when hundreds of city volunteers met a dreadful end at a place called Passchendaele.

During the war, the number of city industries more than doubled, and soldiers returning home barely recognized Toronto as it had become a beehive of industry.

 The city has three museums dedicated to World War I: the Queen's Own Rifles museum at Casa Loma; the 48th Highlanders museum at St. Andrew's Church, 75 Simcoe Street; and the Toronto Scottish Regiment museum at the Fort York Armory, 650 Fleet Street.

WORLD WAR II

The War Machine

On September 1, 1939, Germany marched into Poland, and two days later, both France and Britain declared war, with Canada following suit on September 10. Torontonians were stunned and could hardly believe that the old war had started up again, and for months after the declaration, there was hope for a reprieve. However, when word reached the city that German troops had invaded Norway, Denmark and the Low Countries of Belgium and Holland, residents got ready for a big, long battle. Local industries converted to manufacturing war materials, and new factories were quickly set up to produce guns and munitions. By the end of the conflict, these factories would be supplying almost half of the weapons used by the British and Commonwealth armies.

The Long Branch Arsenal just outside the city produced hundreds of thousands of sten guns and specially modified Lee-Enfield rifles, while the Ingles Company on Strachan Avenue produced more than 300,000 Browning 9mm pistols along with Bren machine guns. Guns aside, Toronto soon became an airplane factory with companies turning out both fighter planes and bombers; the Victory Aircraft Company at Malton turned out 3629 aircraft, including the famous "dam buster" Avro Lancaster Mk Xs, while the De Havilland Company at Malton assembled some 1100 plywood Mosquito fighter bombers.

Bombs Away!

In 1939, not one Canadian company had the expertise or equipment to fuse and fill the bombs and cannon shells that Britain so desperately needed, so the Canadian government decided to construct a plant from scratch. Dubbed "Project 24," the expertise was cobbled together by the Hamilton brothers, two ex-pat Englishmen from the U.S. state of Utah who had founded a company there in 1903 called the General Engineering Company. The building site for the new General Engineering Company (Canada) Limited, affectionately called "Geco" was Scarboro Township, at Toronto's east end, where 2700 construction workers laboured to build 172 buildings with a total floor space of almost 70,000 square metres and over 3050 metres of underground tunnels.

The plant started up in the fall of 1941, and by the summer of 1942, it was at peak production, with 6000 workers assembling and fusing thousands of cannon shells and tracer bullets from parts manufactured by 55 area companies. Geco was immense and operated 24/7 until the war's end. It employed mostly women because Toronto's men were off fighting.

DID YOU KNOW?

In all, Canada contributed 1.1 million fighting men and women to the war effort, with 42,400 killed and 60,000 wounded. In 1942, Toronto city hall began keeping track of the city's war dead, and today, in the city's archives, there are 12 boxes with more than 3300 names and particulars of Torontonians killed in World War II.

Kids Pitching In

During the war years, the kapok used to make naval life vests was in short supply, so Toronto's school children helped by gathering a substitute product from city parks and ravines… milkweed pods.

Our Pilots

The main requirements for a pilot to join the Royal Flying Corps were the ability to shoot straight and drive a car, talents possessed by many young Torontonians. Around one-third of pilots serving in the RFC during World War I were Canadians, with about one-third of those hailing from Toronto and nearby communities.

Toronto contributed more flying aces, those pilots shooting down more than five enemy aircraft, than any city in the Commonwealth. Toronto's own Alfred Atkey, an ace of aces, shot down 33 enemy aircraft.

Bond, James Bond

Although many literary historians attribute the name of Ian Fleming's famous MI5 "licensed to kill" James Bond character to an actual British ornithologist named James Bond, the name more likely derived from St. James Bond United Church at 1066 Avenue Road. During World War II, Ian Fleming trained at the infamous "Camp X" near Whitby, and for part of his training, Fleming lived in Toronto in a house directly across the road from the church.

Toronto Landmarks

I like Toronto a lot, it's a good city. The only thing that really annoys me about Toronto is that you're turning Maple Leaf Gardens into a grocery store, which is absolutely nothing short of disgusting.

—Rick Wakeman,
keyboard player for Yes

ARCHITECTURALLY PLEASING

Unlike the great cities of Europe with their buildings of everlasting quarry stone, buildings of note in Toronto were invariably constructed of cheap-as-dirt wood, with most being obliterated by fire at some point. Even government buildings constructed from stone or brick went up in smoke because their wood framing and interiors proved to be extremely flammable.

In 1850, the city got some sorely needed bylaws to govern construction and the storage of what had become an expected hazard of firefighting, gunpowder. From 1790 to 1830, supplies usually arrived at York in barrels, and the buying of barrelled gunpowder was common enough that citizens fighting fires would approach them with justifiable trepidation. Steamships were infamous for spouting sparks from their smokestacks that started fires, and they were soon required by city bylaw to screen their stacks. However, around that time, another even greater fire starter began to enter the city—the railways with their spark-spewing locomotives, which over the years started blazes that removed entire city blocks. Not until the Great Fire of 1849 did the city look at having a proper firefighting corps with paid members, firehalls, steam-operated pumpers and callboxes, a process that took another two decades to implement to a point where buildings of historical importance had a chance to survive into the future.

Fires aside, many of Toronto's landmark buildings made it into modern times, with a few being mothballed because

historical designation prevented their demolition and the list of improvements demanded by the city to keep them open to the public proved prohibitively expensive.

Toronto has many historical landmarks; the following pages are just a small sampling.

St. Lawrence Market

In 1803, the north side of Front Street north to King, west to Jarvis and east to Church Street was designated a market block for area farmers and fishermen to sell their wares. By 1831, the block was a filthy mess, so the city tore it down and rebuilt it, adding a few brick structures. In 1834, after city incorporation, city council met in a brick market building on the southwest corner of King and Jarvis Streets. Messed up and torn down again in 1844, the block was rebuilt to a design by city architect Henry Bower Lane only to go up in flames in the Great Fire of 1849. In 1850, the city constructed the third market complex across Front Street (its present location) to a design by city architect William Thomas, along with a second three-storey city hall that served as an entrance to the market's side wings. While having undergone many changes to its façade over the years, that edifice is still there, incorporated into today's St. Lawrence Market complex and called St. Lawrence Hall. In 1904, the market's two side wings were demolished and replaced by a huge, steel-reinforced building modelled after London's Victoria Station.

The Flatiron Building

This wedge-shaped building of red-brick construction at the intersections of Front and Wellington Streets replaced a similarly shaped, three-storey, wooden addition of the Wellington Hotel constructed in 1845, which earned the building the nickname "the Coffin Block" for its weird shape. The Coffin Block was thought to have been inspired by a similar structure built in 1830 by a Mister Brown, founder of the Pennsylvania town of

Brownsville, and called "the Flatiron Building" because it was shaped like a clothes iron. That building survives today and must have had some architectural merit because it inspired similarly shaped buildings in other cities, beginning with the Imperial Buildings in Liverpool, England, in 1879.

What was good enough for Liverpool was good enough for George Gooderham, the whisky baron. In 1891, he had the Coffin Block torn down, and in its place, he erected the present building for the offices of the world's foremost distiller of whisky, Gooderham & Worts. The edifice looks taller than its four storeys, and that is the result of a raised foundation and high ceiling floors.

The Gates of Benvenuto

Designed and constructed around 1880 by famous ironworker Benetto Zalaffi of Sienna, Italy, the gates guarded the entrance to the Avenue Road and Edmund Avenue home of millionaire property developer Simeon Henan Janes until its demolition in 1932.

All that remains of Jane's monumental stone mansion is the retaining wall along Avenue Road and the street Benvenuto Place, a name adopted in 1956 by the Benvenuto Place Apartments, now a condominium. Saved from the scrapyard, Zalaffi's wonderful iron gates were dismantled and moved to 40-42 Burton Road in Forest Hill.

The Alexandra Gates

Now marking the north end of the University of Toronto's Philosopher's Walk, a meandering, north-south pathway that follows buried Taddle Creek, the Alexandra Gates originally stood at the corner of Bloor Street and Avenue Road. Constructed by the Imperial Order of the Daughters of the Empire to mark the 1901 visit to Toronto by the Duke and Duchess of Cornwall, later King George V and Queen Mary, the gates were moved to their present location in 1962 to facilitate the widening of Avenue Road.

The Royal Alexandra Theatre

Financed by a group of Toronto's young investors, led by 21-year-old Cawthra Mulock, son of a wealthy city family and owner of a successful iron foundry, the Royal Alex was designed by young Hamilton-born architect John Lyle Macintosh working for the New York firm Carrere and Hastings. The only instruction that Macintosh received from young Mulock was to build "the finest theatre on the continent." The 1500-seat Beaux Arts–style theatre was completed in 1907 and named for Queen Alexandra, wife of King Edward VII, and it was a jewel box surpassing all expectations.

In 1918, the Spanish flu claimed the life of the theatre's young founder, Cawthra Mulock, and management passed entirely to Lawrence "Sol" Solman, who, in 1922, would also serve as the manager of the Sunnyside Amusement Park. During the late '30s, the Royal Alex began to suffer from declining attendance because of the rising popularity of movie houses, a condition that accelerated over the years until the theatre was sold to local department store owner Edward "Ed" Mirvish in 1962 with the stipulation that it be run for another five years. Surprising every-one, Mirvish had the theatre restored and, employing his business acumen, turned it into a paying and popular theatre venue for mostly road-show productions.

The Royal Alex is located at 260 King Street West, with perform-ances and schedules listed online.

Royal Ontario Museum

What you see today is a far cry from the museum that opened its doors to the public in 1914. Back then it was a collection of five separate buildings dedicated to five different endeavours: Archaeology, Paleontology, Mineralogy, Zoology and Geology. Over the years, under the control of the University of Toronto, the buildings were connected, and during the Great Depression of the 1930s, as a make work project, the building was expanded to its present-day architectural magnificence. In 1955, the five museums were reorganized into one entity, the Royal Ontario Museum, or ROM, and in 1968, it was officially separated from the U of T and placed under governorship of the Province of Ontario. The ROM underwent a $55 million dollar renovation in 1978, and in 2007, that awful-looking greenhouse, called the Michael Lee-Chin Crystal, was hung off the west end. However, from the inside the greenhouse takes on a different perspective, and patrons can almost excuse its exterior appearance. Looks aside, the ROM is the best afternoon sojourn in Toronto, and patrons are guaranteed to leave a whole lot smarter then they were when they entered.

Wesley Building

Constructed in 1915 and originally the home of the Methodist Book and Publishing Company, this mammoth structure at Queen and John Street is now occupied by CITY TV and is called the Chum Building. Looking weirdly out of place, this white stone structure is notable for its many terra cotta architectural embellishments and gargoyles, one of which bears an uncanny resemblance to former CHUM whip Moses Znaimer.

Eaton's College Street

Conceived in the early 1920s as an Art Deco Eaton's flagship store, the project was to feature a skyscraper office complex meant to rival New York City's famed Chrysler Building. Construction began in 1928 and was completed in 1930, but with only the first stage, seven-storey building constructed because of Depression-era financial restraints and problems caused by the underground watercourse of Taddle Creek.

Toronto lost a skyscraper but gained an exquisite Art Deco shopping experience along with the seventh-floor public rooms, the famous Eaton Auditorium and the Round Room Restaurant, both designed by famed French artist and designer Jean Carlu. Sealed up in 1977, when Eaton sold the store, the seventh floor was completely refurbished in 2003 and is now an events venue and supper club called the Carlu.

Bata Shoe Museum

While her husband, Thomas, was on his way to becoming shoemaker to the world, Sonja Bata collected icons of his trade—shoes. Beginning in the late 1940s, wherever Thomas travelled to set up his Bata Shoe Company factories, Sonja went along to search the markets and antique shops for the best examples of traditional footwear. In 1979, Thomas grew tired of sharing his home with Sonja's thousands of carefully preserved and boxed shoes and convinced her to move them into an empty wing of his office building in the Don Mills area of Toronto. They called it the Bata Shoe Museum Foundation and hired a curator. Not much of a museum, it had few visitors so in June 1992, Sonja, as CEO of the foundation, had the whole shebang moved to the second floor of the Colonnade building on Bloor Street, in Toronto's busiest commercial area. A better venue, but not by much, and all the while Sonja was adding to the collection. Deciding the collection needed a proper home, Sonja put out feelers to acquire property; when a lot at the nearby corner of Bloor and St. George Street became available, she pounced. As the architect to design her dream she chose Raymond Moriyama, who upon touring the Colonnade museum knew exactly what Sonja wanted to house her collection—a shoebox, not too obvious, but still a shoebox with a definable not-quite-closed lid.

The museum is great; it does not smell like dirty feet, and it displays all manner of traditional footwear: prehistoric, Native American and those worn by almost every culture on the planet. An afternoon of shoes is a not-to-be-missed opportunity for both tourists and Torontonians, if only to see the shoes worn by famous celebrities, and yes…Elvis is in the house.

CN Tower

At 553.3 metres it is not the world's tallest building, as many of its more than two million visitors suppose; it is the world's tallest tower. Those visitors also suppose the CN stands for Canadian National, the railway concern that built the tower; it does not—it stands for Canada's National Tower, a 1995 rename by the people that bought the tower, the Canadian government. That the tower was purposely built to be the world's tallest is also a misconception; decisions to that end were made as the design process progressed.

Originally designed as a concrete tripod structure topped by a steel frame for the support of radio and television transmission antennas, the concept was in constant flux almost to the start of construction on February 6, 1973. That it was built at all was a result of the times; with no communication satellites there was a need for downward radio and television transmission to counter interference from the many tall buildings in the city's core. Also, Canadian National Railway, a major supporter of the ill-fated Metro Centre, wanted the tower to be an iconic emblem to the might of their company, and its location was chosen to head up that development like the prow ornament on a great ship. The scrapping of the Metro Centre plan, which would have seen Toronto's waterfront looking like Venice, left the CN tower isolated and almost impossible to access until the city provided the Skywalk and tunnels in 1989.

Nowadays the tower centres a vast sea of condominiums and is an easy reach by tourists who love to ride the six elevators (one has a glass bottom) to the glass-bottomed observation deck at the top. Once they are on the glass deck, many patrons discover their latent acrophobia, causing them to retire to the world's highest revolving restaurant and procure a bottle from the world's highest wine cellar.

Most visitors, including Torontonians, were unaware the tower is hollow until the world's longest metal staircase (2579 steps) was moved inside, a move that took away some of the panache from the annual race to the top on the two days a year the tower allows access to the stairs for charity events. If participants are fit, the usual time to the top is around 30 minutes, but the record is 7 minutes and 52 seconds.

In March 2007, the tower stopped being a benign icon and turned to bombarding the city with blocks of ice loosed from the pod by high winds, causing sections of the city to be closed to vehicular traffic. This singular incident caused a slight re-emergence of the doomsayer brigade, a headline-grabbing group that predicted catastrophe should Toronto be shaken by a major earthquake. Toppling over was a popular topic during construction when newspapers would feature maps of the predicted devastation on their front page. A bit far-fetched as the tower's foundation is over 15 metres deep, but a tiny segment of the doomsayers—those who predicted dire consequences for migrating birds—proved correct and until the lights were turned off during migrations, the tower required an early morning sweep up of an astronomical number of dead birds. Birds still die, but the numbers are no longer astronomical.

Toronto's CN Tower has become a major tourist venue and features a breathtaking elevator ride to four observation levels, the famous 360 Degree Restaurant, a 3D movie experience and a shopping arcade. Tickets are required for the elevator ride but are free for restaurant diners with reservations, though an extra ticket must be purchased to reach the top.

Public Sculpture

They are everywhere in Toronto; the earlier ones are made of bronze and are raised high above the ground, but newer examples are usually constructed of steel, aluminum or concrete with a few designed to be interactive, like an adult playground accoutrement. Most have been sadly neglected or have had the artist's intent blunted by condominium blight and the changing times, such as the Airmen's Memorial on University Avenue, now affectionately known as "Gumby Goes to Heaven" because that is exactly what it looks like. At the bottom of that same University Avenue sits a large corkscrew installation that is dear to my heart because I watched its painful two-year-long construction in a Yorkville parking lot and was present the day an errant truck made its reconstruction necessary.

The Sundial Folly on Lake Shore Boulevard is an interactive work that, even though neglected, is still fun and allows people to get inside. Although the artists' intended view of the lake is now blocked by an ugly condominium, the sundial still tells the time. For temporary installations, weird and otherwise, there is the Toronto Sculpture Garden at 115 King Street East, where both Torontonians and visitors can view contemporary installations from 8:00 AM to sundown.

DID YOU  KNOW?

The University of Toronto occupies property leased to the city for 999 years by the estate of William Dummer Powell, the fifth Chief Justice of Upper Canada. Queen's Park, the site of Ontario's legislative building, is constructed on land subleased from the University of Toronto.

FAMOUS ABODES

Mackenzie House

Once the home of Sir Francis Bond Head, the chief protagonist in William Lyon Mackenzie's failed rebellion of 1837, the house would ironically become home to the former mayor, newspaper publisher and political rabble-rousing William Lyon Mackenzie himself. The circa-1830 Greek-revival brick rowhouse has been completely refurbished and operates as a museum replete with printing press and odds and ends from the era. The house is also a favourite of spook hunters because it is supposedly one of the most haunted edifices in Toronto.

Mackenzie House is located at 82 Bond Street. It is well worth the small admission charged.

Casa Loma

Major-General Sir Henry Mill Pellatt's fabulous "castle on the hill" was designed by city architect E.J. Lennox and completed in 1914, only to be seized by the city for unpaid taxes in 1925. In 1927, Casa Loma became a fashionable hotel until the Great Depression caused its failure. It remained boarded up until 1937, when it became a museum operated by the Kiwanis Club of West Toronto. During World War II, the stables of Casa Loma were used as a factory for assembling bombsights and radar devices, with parts delivered secretly by bread trucks. Secret passages, tunnels, a conservatory, stables, a marvellous garden and the odd ghost sighting—the castle on the hill has it all.

DID YOU KNOW?

In 1899, during one of Toronto's cyclical economic depressions, downtown Bloor Street homes situated on property of considerable size could be purchased for around $2000. In 2011, the same property, if available, would cost a purchaser around $20 million.

During the 18th century and part of the 19th, wood was so cheap and plentiful in Toronto that black walnut was often used for fence posts.

OTHER IMPORTANT HERITAGE LANDMARKS

Allan Gardens
Argus Corporation Building
The Beaches
The Beardmore Building
Colborne Lodge
Distillery District
Edwards Gardens
Elgin Theatre
The First Post Office
Fort York
Massey Hall
New City Hall
Old City Hall
Osgoode Hall

Pantages Theatre (now the Canon Theatre)
Queen's Park
Queen's Quay Terminal
R.C. Harris Water Treatment Plant
Spadina House
St. Michael's Cathedral
Todmorden Mills
Toronto Stock Exchange
Union Station
University of Toronto
Wheat Sheaf Tavern
Winter Garden Theatre

Haunted Toronto

I think that we need to get along together if we want to survive in the twenty-first century.

—Sarah Polley, actress

SPOOKY SITES

People see them all the time; there is even an organization to investigate ghostly sightings—the Toronto and Ontario Ghosts and Haunting Research Society. These folks have a detailed website of places you can go if you are looking for a spooky experience.

University College

One of the best sites in Toronto for a thrilling experience, ghost sighting or not, is U of T's University College where a reminder of the demise of stonemason Ivan Reznikoff by methods most foul is slashed into a doorway for all to see. Reznikoff, a Russian, was planning to marry a local lass, but after discovering she was planning to run off with a fellow stone worker, a Greek chap named Diabolos, Reznikoff attacked Diabolos with an axe, hence the slash in the door. Not a man to take being attacked lightly, Diabolos stuck Reznikoff with a knife and supposedly buried his body in the stonework. The story was lent some credence when, years later, a fire exposed the dried-out bones of an unidentified corpse. Reznikoff's ghost has been spotted many times, usually by students after a night of partying, but now and then by a more responsible adult.

St. Michael's Hospital

This site is prime for ghost finding, with a restless spirit dubbed "Sister Vinnie" wandering halls, turning lights on and off and frightening the wits out of nurses, sometimes so badly they are forced to work in pairs.

The Distillery District

The wandering spirit here is James Wort who threw himself down the well after his wife died and his giant windmill failed to work properly. Thrill-seekers have a good chance of seeing

James, especially after imbibing at one of the distillery's great bars. I have seen him, I think, and only after three drinks, so four or five will pretty much guarantee a sighting.

The Keg Steakhouse

Originally built during the mid-1800s by Lord William McMaster, founder of Hamilton's McMaster University, the house was sold 10 years later to Hart Massey, founder of the Massey Ferguson Company. It is the place where his daughter Lillian fell victim to cholera and died. Lots of patrons and staff have seen Lillian, as well as a little boy who runs around the hallways laughing.

The Royal York Hotel

The Royal York has several resident ghosts. Guests often complain of ghostly children running and playing in the hallways, and there is the famous "man in the purple jacket," the ghost of a grey-haired old man who wanders about on the hotel's eighth floor and is often seen by both guests and hotel employees. With 40 million guests over the life of the hotel, one has to expect a few spooks and there are many at the Royal York, most the result of people having committed suicide.

Famous Torontonians

*It's a beautiful city, and the waterfront area is fantastic.
I haven't had time to visit the theatre, but I find it remark-
able that Toronto has the third-largest English-speaking
theatre district in the world, after New York and London.
I once noticed a fellow sitting on a bench, then I realized it
was a statue of Glenn Gould. It's very realistic.*

–Donald Trump, American business magnate

CITY LUMINARIES

In 1996, a star honouring Toronto entrepreneur and theatre impresario Ed Mirvish was set into the sidewalk on King Street West, creating the first of what was intended to be Toronto's Walk of Fame to commemorate its many famous citizens. However, too many thumbs got into the pie, and Toronto's Walk of Fame became Canada's Walk of Fame, resulting in so many stars that it dimmed the tribute intended for Toronto's many luminaries. The city has so many star-worthy luminaries that they could fill a book, but because space is limited, here are just a few that shine as bright as stars on a sidewalk.

Sir Casamir Gzowski (1813–98)

Deported to the U.S. after the abortive 1830 Polish uprising against Russian authority, Gzowski learned first law and then engineering, and applied his skills to building canals and roads. In 1841, Gzowski journeyed to Kingston in a bid to acquire the Welland Canal building contract, and though he failed in that respect, he so impressed Governor Charles Bagot that he was offered and accepted the position of Superintendent of Roads and Waterways for the Hamilton area. Gzowski built roads, canals and the harbours of Port Stanley and Rondeau. In 1845, working mostly out of Toronto, he joined a mining syndicate to explore and develop copper mines.

In 1849, the passage of the Guarantee Act by the province opened up opportunities for railways, and Gzowski was hired by St. Lawrence and Atlantic Railway director Alexander Galt to run a rail line from Toronto to Sarnia. That led to other lucrative railway contracts, and, in 1854, Gzowski & Company won the contract to build the Toronto Esplanade; however, the deal fell apart because of accusations of contract padding, and Gzowski and Alexander Galt parted ways. Undaunted, Gzowski & Company soldiered on, building more rail lines and acquiring various waterfront businesses: cotton, whale oil, an iron rolling mill and the Rossin Hotel.

In 1870, Sir Casamir performed his engineering swan song, the building of the railway bridge across the Niagara River. In 1879, after serving both the federal and provincial governments in various advisory roles, Gzowski was appointed aide-de-camp to Queen Victoria and was knighted in 1890.

Cornelia de Grassi (1814–85)

Filippo "Phillip" de Grassi, an Italian officer serving in the Grand Army of France, was captured by British forces during an early battle of the Peninsula War, Napoleon's ill-fated 1804–14 attempt to subjugate Portugal. Taken to England and paroled, de Grassi obtained a captaincy in the York Light Infantry Volunteers in 1812 and served out his contract in the British West Indies. Returning to England in 1815, he taught languages, got married and had two daughters, Cornelia and Charlotte. In 1831, taking advantage of land grants available to British officers, he took his family to York and settled on a section of land on the east side of the Don River not far from the Todmorden Mills, where he planted apple orchards.

Officers with land grants, especially those with Freemasonry affiliation like de Grassi, were expected to contribute time to militia duty, and de Grassi devoted himself so fully to the task that he was made privy to intrigues against the Upper Canada government of Sir Francis Bond Head by the politically discontented William Lyon Mackenzie. In 1937, word arrived at York that well-armed Mackenzie supporters were gathering from around the province at Montgomery's Tavern north of the city and preparing to march on the city. The news put Governor Bond Head into a panic because all the British military forces had been sent to Lower Canada to put down revolts, and he was left with only a small militia unit, Phillip de Grassi's men.

Governor Bond Head prepared to abandon the city but was convinced to wait while de Grassi reconnoitred the enemy's strength, a difficult task because Yonge Street, the only road to Montgomery's Tavern, was barricaded at several places. De Grassi needed to get spies into the very centre of Mackenzie's mob, and that seemed so impossible a task that Governor Bond Head ordered a ship made ready to depart at a moment's notice. However, providence interceded when de Grassi's daughters got word from a friend working at the Todmorden paper mill that Mackenzie had ordered paper to be delivered to Montgomery's Tavern.

"We can take it," said Cornelia and Charlotte. "We know the area, and who would suspect two girls delivering paper."

Having no alternative, de Grassi agreed, but only allowed his youngest daughter and better rider, Cornelia, to make the attempt. The girl left the paper mill at first light and rode up Yonge Street, passing through rebel roadblocks with little difficulty. After delivering the paper, she got a good look at the rebels and determined that they were completely unprepared for a battle. They were too lightly armed, half drunk and without rations. This was information she had to get to her father, but there was a problem. Mackenzie had issued orders that once in, nobody should be allowed to leave.

In spite of the danger, Cornelia took to her horse, and keeping low in the saddle rode, hell for leather through a hail of bullets into Toronto history. Her report that the rebels were poorly armed, drunk and hungry stopped Bond Head's exodus from Toronto and sent de Grassi's militia north to hold the rebel advance until help arrived from Hamilton.

DID YOU  KNOW?

The name Montgomery would return to haunt captured members of William Lyon Mackenzie's failed insurrection of 1837. Defeated at Montgomery's Tavern on Yonge Street, captured rebels were tried for treason at the magistrate's court on the second floor of Montgomery's Inn on Dundas Street. Although both Montgomerys were Irish, they were not related.

Theodore August Heintzman (1817–99)

Theodore Heintzman, a German piano maker, brought his family to New York City from Berlin in 1850, moved to Buffalo, New York, around 1852 and arrived in Toronto some time in 1860 to avoid the American Civil War and creditors. After constructing his first small pianos in the back room of his son-in-law's house on Duke Street, Heintzman moved his operation in 1866 to a factory at the Junction. Calling his new enterprise Heintzman & Company, he began to manufacture grand and player pianos that sold like hotcakes and made him an extremely wealthy man. In 1889, he constructed a fine home, which he called "The Birches," at the Junction on Annette Street. The house is still standing today with a fully renovated exterior along with modern internal modifications wrought by a property developer.

Sir William Mackenzie (1849–1923)

Born in Kirkfield, a small village on the Talbot River just east of Lake Simcoe, Sir William Mackenzie received an early entrepreneurial education selling rail ties to the Midland Railway. That led to his owning a local grist and sawmill and to more small rail-laying contracts, and eventually to laying tracks in western Canada for the Canadian Pacific Railway (CPR). In 1890, he arrived in Toronto a wealthy man and joined George Kiely and others to buy the Toronto Street Railway. Some months later, Kiely resigned as president of the trolley line, and Sir William took over the position. He quickly turned what had been an almost bankrupt concern into a paying proposition called the Toronto Railway Company, or the TRC.

Timber had led Sir William into the railway business, just as the electrical needs of his streetcars would lead him into the business of electricity. Sir William bought the Electric Development Company, the main Niagara Falls hydro-generating company, set up the Toronto Power Company to get the electricity to Toronto, and then the Toronto Electric Light Company to distribute that electricity to customers. In 1885, he rolled several suburban streetcar companies into his Electric Light Company and formed the Toronto and York Radial Railway, the city's first interurban network of streetcar routes.

In 1887, Sir William bought "Benvenuto," the magnificent mansion built by real estate developer Simeon H. James, but he was always in some faraway place developing new ventures, including the Canadian Northern Railway and new electrical systems in countries such as Brazil, where his efforts sowed the seeds of the mighty Brascan empire and got him knighted in 1911. In 1918, he lost the Canadian Northern Railway to a federal expropriation and, in the early 1920s, during what city politicians called the "Clean Up Deal," Sir William's business creations within the city were expropriated. The city got the Toronto Railway Company, the Toronto Electric Light Company and the Toronto York Radial Railway, and Sir William got $11.5 million of taxpayer's money through an arbitration award.

Charles Vance Millar (1853–1926)

Toronto resident Charles Millar chose law as a profession, and though that proved successful, he made most of his considerable fortune from investments in British Columbia real estate ventures. Unmarried, affable, with a lifelong penchant for pranks, Millar shocked Toronto society by leaving a will that contained more than a few practical jokes. He left shares in the Ontario Jockey Club to two socially prominent Torontonians who had publicly condemned the sport, and a similar number of shares to a man who had been denied Jockey Club membership for having a less-than-staunch reputation. His shares in the O'Keefe Brewing Company, a Catholic-owned business, were willed to Protestant ministers and Orange Order members, and a house in Jamaica was left to three lawyers who hated each other.

However, his biggest joke lay in clause 9 of his will, wherein he left the bulk of his estate to the woman who could bear the most children in a 10-year period. The initial amount was $100,000; however, by the time the contest had run its course in 1936, the value of the shares in the estate had risen to an astounding $750,000. Legal battles ensued, but in the end, four women received $125,000 each for bearing nine children, with the remainder going to lawyers' fees and to settle various lawsuits from spurious claimants.

Edward "Ned" Hanlan (1855–1908)

Bootlegger, hotelier and one of the greatest sports figures of the 19th century, Ned Hanlan, the "boy in blue" and world-champion single-sculls rower put Toronto on the world map. His father, John Hanlan, one of the Toronto Islands' earliest residents and its first constable, had constructed a small hotel on the peninsula's eastern tip, at a place that became known as Hanlan's Point. By order of Toronto City Council, no alcoholic beverages were allowed on the Toronto Islands, but that meant few customers, so John Hanlan defied the law and offered clients a full bar of bootlegged spirits. His youngest son, Ned, was the bootlegger and got in plenty of rowing practice ferrying cases of whisky from the mainland. Ned also rowed back and forth to school, fetched groceries for the hotel and pretty much spent all of his time at the oars. That was fine by Ned, and he got very good at rowing, a tremendously popular spectator sport in those days. Soon he was beating all comers at Island regattas.

In 1873, Ned won the championship of Toronto Bay, and, the following year, wearing his trademark blue shirt and red headband for the first time, Ned beat famous Ontario sculler Thomas Loudan in a race that featured a side bet of $100. The next year, he won the Ontario championship and even more money from side bets. The sport was now attracting sizeable prize money and side bets, and that caught the attention of Toronto businessmen. They formed a syndicate to back Ned's ambition to be the world's best and make big money in the process.

Ned won all his races, earning a small fortune for himself and a large one for his syndicate, but, in 1878, the large fortune became obscene when a group of wealthy Torontonians wagered $300,000 (about $30 million today) on Ned's bid to become United States champion. That he won handily earned him a hero's reception on his return to Toronto. The next year, he defeated the English champion and got another hero's welcome. However, his welcome of welcomes occurred in 1880 after he defeated Australian E.A. Trikett for the world championship.

Ned Hanlan would go on to win another 300 matches, losing only six, and is memorialized by an appreciative public in a statue on Hanlan's Point, near to where he constructed his famous Hanlan's Hotel in 1880.

DID YOU KNOW?

James Earl Ray, confessed assassin of famed civil rights leader Dr. Martin Luther King Jr., lived at a rooming house on the west side of Ossington Avenue north of Queen Street for several weeks after committing his foul deed on April 4, 1968. While residing in Toronto, on his way to England where he was captured, Ray used the alias Eric S. Galt, a name he probably adopted from the city of Galt, Ontario. Sentenced to 99 years, the confessed murderer would later recant his confession, claiming a plot was instigated by then FBI director Herbert Hoover. His conspiracy claim actually had some merit, and his case was reviewed by the U.S. government but later dismissed as nonsense. James Earl Ray died of liver failure in 1998, still claiming to be Hoover's innocent dupe.

Major-General Sir Henry Mill Pellatt
(1859–1939)

After graduating from Upper Canada College, Pellatt worked as a clerk in his father's successful investment company, becoming a full partner in 1883. That same year, he bought control of the Toronto Electric Light Company from founder J.J. Wright and invested in Niagara Falls power projects. By 1892, and in full control of his father's investment company, Pellatt's speculations turned to railways, banks and land, investments that proved so successful that by 1900, he controlled 25 percent of Canada's economy. The high point of Pellatt's life occurred in 1905, when he received a knighthood for his role as commanding officer and chief financial benefactor of the Queen's Own Rifles, a city militia unit.

Pellatt had the golden touch in business, and with so much money rolling in, he decided to make good on a promise to his wife, Lady Mary, to build her a castle. He hired famed Toronto architect E.J. Lennox, who completed the project in 1914. The Pellatts spared no expense in furnishing their "castle on the hill," or Casa Loma.

During World War I, Sir Henry had many of his companies nationalized, for which he received no compensation. After the war, Canada fell into an economic depression, and Sir Henry's investments soured. He lost $2 million in the collapse of the Home Bank of Canada, and with money scarce, Sir Henry lost Casa Loma to the city to pay back taxes.

In 1929, Pellatt was broke and homeless, so his former chauffeur took him in. Sir Henry Pellatt, once the wealthiest man in Toronto, died in 1939 with $200 in his pocket and owning only the clothes on his back.

David A. Dunlap (1863–1924)

Dunlap was born poor but died very rich, and in between, he used the wealth he acquired from gold mines in Timmins and Cobalt to buy 243 hectares west of the Don River and south of York Mills Road. In 1914, he and wife Jessie Donalda Bell emulated Hart Massey's son, Walter, who had opened City Dairy in 1900, and established Donalda Farms, a dairy farm that, for the times, was something of a miracle.

Hundreds of Guernsey cows lived in scrupulously clean tiled barns munching the best fodder money could buy while listening to piped-in classical music. Mothers giving kids milk from Donalda Farms no longer feared diseases, and the farm prospered like no other until the area was subdivided in the 1950s for home construction.

Even after contributing millions to the Toronto General Hospital and the Art Gallery of Ontario, Dunlap left an estate worth more than $6 million, and in the vernacular of the day, that weren't hay. His home on Donalda Crescent that once overlooked verdant cow pastures is now the clubhouse of the Donalda Golf and Country Club and overlooks a verdant fairway.

Thomas John "Tommy" Thomson
(1877–1917)

He went north to paint and stayed to become a mystery. One of the greats of Canadian art, Tommy Thomson was an enigma in life as well as in death. In 1912, while working at Grip Limited, a Toronto typesetting and lithography company that employed four artists who would go on to become members of the Group of Seven (Frederick Varley, Franklin Carmichael, Frank Johnston and J.E.H. MacDonald), he was advised by the artists to head north for landscape inspiration. In 1913, Tommy took the train up to a little station in Algonquin Provincial Park called Joe Lake. From that point on, his artwork took on a whole new dimension, a naturalness soon recognized by his fellow artists including Lawren Harris, who invited Tommy into his sponsored Toronto studio at 25 Severn Street (the present-day Studio Building, a National Historic Site). In 1914, Tommy tried to enlist as a war artist along with Varley and A.Y. Jackson but was refused. He consoled himself by moving to Joe Lake Station, where he produced his best works—until the summer of 1917, when his body was found in Canoe Lake, legs wrapped in copper fishing line and head badly bruised.

The coroner called it death by drowning and thought Tommy had hooked onto a big lake trout and, during the excitement, had stood up in the canoe, tangled his legs in fishing line and fallen into the water, striking his head on a rock. None of the locals believed the verdict; Tommy had been too good with a rod and was so expert a canoeist that he would never have stood up or gotten his feet tangled. It was a mystery, one that got even deeper after Tommy's family had his remains dug up and moved to his hometown of Leith, Ontario. Many people did not believe that the remains had actually been moved, and years later an interested Justice of the Peace named William Little poked around in what had been Tommy's grave and found another body, that of a Cree person who, like Tommy, had a cracked skull. Because all that remained were bones, it is likely the second body was in the grave before Tommy.

Although many locals believe Tommy was murdered by Martin Bletcher, a local man of German extraction and the same man who reported Tommy's overturned canoe, it is just speculation. (Bletcher and Tommy had argued about the war the night before Tommy's disappearance.)

Another theory is that Tommy got into a fight with hotel owner Shannon Fraser over money owed to Tommy. Fraser struck Tommy, causing him to fall and hit his head on a fire grate. After realizing the fall had killed his adversary, Fraser with help from his wife, Anne, hauled Tommy's body to his canoe, wrapped his legs in fishing line and, with Anne following in another canoe, overturned Tommy's craft in a remote part of Canoe Lake. While this scenario is also speculation, it does carry some weight, as it was Anne Fraser's deathbed confession to a friend.

The mysterious death of one of Canada's foremost artists has been the subject of several books and film documentaries and will probably never be solved to satisfaction. However, it has added some mystique to Canoe Lake—every season canoeists report being followed by the grey spectre of Tommy Thompson's canoe-paddling ghost.

Mary Pickford (1898–1979)

Born to the Smith family on April 8, 1892, "Baby" Gladys Smith would be on stage at the nearby Princess Theatre by age five and would spend the next nine years playing Shea's Theatre in Toronto and travelling the northwestern U.S. vaudeville circuit with her manager mother, younger brother and sister. At age 15, she walked into the New York office of famous producer David Belasco and demanded a job. Belasco agreed, but only if she changed her name to Mary Pickford, and, in 1907, she opened on Broadway in a Belasco play called *The Warrens of Virginia*.

In 1909, entranced by a new media called "motion pictures," she went to see American Biograph producer D.W. Griffith and asked for a part in a picture. She got it that afternoon and was asked to return the following day for another role, for which she would be paid $5, the same as all of Griffith's actors.

"Mister Griffith," said Mary, "I'm a Belasco actress and an artist. I must have $10." She got her $10, but Griffith made her do a film every week, and like all Griffith actors, she got no billing. In 1910, she accompanied Griffith to California where she secretly married fellow Biograph actor Owen Moore.

The next year, Pickford left Biograph and went to work for producer Carl Laemmie doing one-reelers for more money and star billing. Thirty-five films later, she broke her contract and returned to Biograph to do some of her best work—and get star billing. In 1912, David Belasco offered Mary a part playing the little blind girl in *A Good Little Devil*, a play that fledging producer Adolph Zukor wanted to make into a film. Zukor would call his film company "Famous Players in Famous Plays," the precursor to the Famous Players theatre chain.

Mary made 21 films for Zukor under his new banner "Paramount Pictures," and, by 1916, she was making $150,000 per year as the most popular actress in the world. She had a new two-year contract with Zukor by the end of 1916 that had her making her own films for her own company, Pickford Films, under the Paramount umbrella, for which she made $1 million. The highlight of this venture was her production of *Rebecca of Sunnybrook Farm*.

While she was campaigning for war bond sales with Charlie Chaplin and Douglas Fairbanks Jr., Mary and Douglas fell in love, and while they waited for their divorces, they, along with Chaplin, formed United Artists, for which she made her second best grossing film, *Little Lord Fauntleroy*. She and Fairbanks were married in 1921 and lived happily for many years at their Hollywood mansion "Pickfair," until alcohol use took a toll on them both, ending in a 1936 divorce.

In 1928, Pickford and other actors formed the Academy of Motion Pictures with its accompanying Oscar award, and Mary's first talking picture, *The Taming of the Shrew*, earned her the first award for the best female role. Mary lived on at Pickfair, becoming the Hollywood "hostess with the mostest," and, in 1937, she married actor-musician Charles "Buddy" Rogers, a relationship that endured until her death in 1979.

DID YOU KNOW?

Edwin Alonzo Boyd, leader of the infamous Boyd Gang of bank robbers, was cornered and captured in Toronto on March 15, 1952, while living in a house at 42 Heath Street West. Boyd gave up without a fight but was detained in the house for almost an hour to allow then-mayor Allan Lamport to arrive and be photographed helping with the arrest. On September 8, 1952, Boyd and three of his gang members escaped from the Don Jail but were recaptured on September 16, hiding in a North York barn.

Edward Samuel "Ted" Rogers (1900–39)

Ted Rogers parents' were told that their frail son would not survive more than a few years, and though he did die a young man at age 39, that was time enough for him to become one of Canada's wealthiest citizens through what he called his "tools of success"—hard work and dedication. His passion was radio, and when he happened to see a demonstration of a new type of radio vacuum tube in 1924, he immediately got a licence for Canada and began to manufacture and distribute lightweight radios. In 1927, he founded the iconic CFRB radio station, and, in 1933, he and wife Velma had a son, Edward Samuel "Ted" Rogers Jr.—the boy who grew up to be the master of Canada's airwaves.

Edward "E.P." Taylor (1901–89)

Born in Ottawa, E.P. Taylor graduated from McGill University in 1922. He then parlayed a family beer business into an industrial empire that included Canadian Breweries Corporation, Massey-Harris, Orange Crush, Canadian Food Products, Standard Chemical, Domtar Paper, Dominion Stores, Standard Broadcasting and Hollinger Mines. However, Taylor is best known to Torontonians for his Windfields Farm racehorse-breeding endeavour that gave Canada the king of racehorses, Northern Dancer. Although not a native Torontonian, Taylor qualifies as a favourite son because his principle residence during his most successful years was Windfields Estate at 2489 Bayview Avenue, now operated as the Canadian Film Centre.

During the early 1960s, Taylor constructed the Lyford Quay housing and golf course project in the Bahamas and retired to that epitome of gracious living. In 1973, Taylor came out of retirement and took over International Housing Limited, and, by 1978, he was building low-cost housing in 40 countries around the world.

Edward "E.P." Taylor passed away in 1989 at the age 88 at Lyford Quay. I was in the Simpsons store on that day and can remember people toasting his accomplishments with orange drinks from the Honeydew stand, a brand name acquired by Taylor in 1943 and ubiquitous in Toronto for generations.

Frank Gehry (1929–)

Frank Gehry was born Ephraim Owen Goldberg on February 28, 1929, at his grandparent's house at 15 Beverly Street, near his first Canadian architectural undertaking—the redesign of the Art Gallery of Ontario. In 1947, Frank and his parents moved to Los Angeles, where his father changed the family's name to Gehry before they applied for U.S. citizenship. Frank adopted his first name a few years later.

Enrolled at L.A. City College, Frank took an architectural course as an incidental but soon became so enthralled by the subject that he managed to earn a scholarship to the University of Southern California, from which he graduated with a degree in architecture in 1954. For the next eight years, Frank bounced around; he worked for several firms, got married, took courses, did a stint in the army, had two kids and spent a year working in Paris before returning to Los Angeles in 1964 to open his own firm, Gehry Associates. For a number of years, Frank designed conventional buildings, but by the end of the 1970s, he was moving away from the conventional into more imaginative designs, with projects such as the California Aerospace Museum and the Loyola University Law School building.

During the 1980s, Frank concentrated on designing for international clients, and, in 1989, he received the Pritzker Architecture Prize, the highest award in architecture. In 1990, his design for the Weisman Art Museum at the University of Minnesota launched Gehry into architectural stardom, especially after completion of his Guggenheim Museums in Bilbao, Spain, and Abu Dhabi, United Arab Emirates, and his tour de force Walt Disney Concert Hall in downtown L.A.

Along the path to stardom, Gehry also created designs for watches, furniture, liquor bottles and the World Cup of Hockey trophy. An architect for all seasons is Frank Gehry, and in what he described as an emotional experience, he returned home to give Torontonians a fusion of light, wood and his wonderful imagination in the new Art Gallery of Ontario.

Glenn Herbert Gould (1932–82)

Our troubled maestro of the 88 keys was born Glenn Herbert Gold, but the Gold family changed their name to Gould in 1939, at about the time Glenn began to show promise as a child music prodigy. The kid had perfect pitch and could already read music like a book, so off he went to study at Toronto's Royal Conservatory of Music, where he absorbed all they could teach him and became a professional pianist at only 13 years old. In 1946 he played with the Toronto Symphony, followed a year later by a solo recital he repeated in 1950 on CBC radio, an occasion that so enamoured him to the media that he would give up doing recitals in 1969 to concentrate on radio and recording. In total, he performed on stage about 200 times, during which he progressively became more eccentric: insisting halls be heated to 26°C, wearing winter clothing in summer, developing hypochondria, eschewing public appearances and driving orchestra conductors mad with his weird body movements and tempo variations. In 1955, he gave his first American recital at the Town Hall in New York City and the next day received a recording contract from Columbia Records.

In 1967, Gould began a five-year affair with noted U.S. sculptress and painter Cornelia Foss, wife of the composer Lukas Foss. Although she moved to Toronto into a rented house at 110 St. Clair Avenue, her paramour became convinced Lukas Foss would try to poison him and refused to join her, preferring the security of his nearby apartment. Cornelia Foss would later describe her time with Gould as being overly sexual with interludes of extreme paranoia. Along with his increasing paranoia, Gould became more of a hypochondriac, taking all kinds of prescribed medications for what was revealed after his autopsy to be mostly imagined pains and aliments.

On September 27, 1982, complaining of a severe headache and a gradual numbness in his extremities, Glenn Gould was admitted to Toronto General Hospital where the numbness, diagnosed as a stroke but looking suspiciously like curare poisoning, continued to spread despite treatment, ending his weird and wonderful life just a week past his 50th birthday.

Melvin Douglas "Mel" Lastman (1933–)

They call it the "Lastman political era"—those years from 1997 to 2003 when Torontonians got to watch a Bad Boy commercial become a reality show. Torontonians already knew Mel could sell just about anything with all the media attention he generated; hardly a day passed when Mel's sales theatrics didn't grab some free advertising. But hardly anyone thought he would sell himself to the voting populace and become mayor of the megacity in 1997.

Mel belonged to Toronto; he started out selling appliances on College Street in 1949 calling himself "Mr. Laundry," a name he soon changed to "Bad Boy" before opening the first Bad Boy furniture store in 1955. Ever the promoter, Mel journeyed to the Arctic—"Just had to sell a refrigerator to an Eskimo," he said—gave away money on street corners, was involved in the "was she or wasn't she" kidnapping of his wife and dressed in outlandish costumes, including the famous prison stripes. He won a seat on North York Board of Control in 1969, and in 1975, he sold his Bad Boy stores and made an unsuccessful try for a seat on the Provincial Legislature. With no more Bad Boy appliances to sell and his political life stifled, Mel decided to sell North York, a task he performed admirably until the city was amalgamated into the megacity and the Lastman era began in Toronto.

In 1991, his son Blayne relaunched the Bad Boy chain and tried a redux of his dad's sales pitch but he looked too comfortable in prison stripes, forcing dad to make cameo appearances, and Torontonians got a double dose of Mayor Mel and his famous "Noooobody" quip. They also got those weird commercials that featured President Bill Clinton doing the "Noooobody," which continued in spite of warnings of legal action from the U.S. Whitehouse, a defiance that endeared Mel to Torontonians. Overall, and despite his many faux pas—such as calling in the military for snow removal in 1999 while on vacation in Florida—Torontonians liked Mayor Mel and could forgive him for almost anything. They could forgive him for not minding the till as a billion dollars went out the windows of city hall during the computer/phone scandal and various property sell-offs. They could even forgive his famous "cannibal gaffe" when in 2001, before flying off to promote Toronto's bid for the 2008 games to the Olympics Committee meeting in Kenya, Mayor Mel's natural effervescence betrayed him when he jokingly told reporters he could see himself in a pot of boiling water surrounded by dancing natives. The little guy in prison stripes retired from politics in 2003 and returned to running the Bad Boy stores, where at various times customers are treated to a personal sales pitch by Mister Bad Boy himself, former mayor Mel Lastman.

Edward Samuel "Ted" Rogers Jr.
(1933–2008)

In 1960, while still a student at Osgoode Law School, Ted Rogers Jr. jumped into specialty radio by buying radio station CHFI, a pioneer of FM radio. In 1965, he pioneered himself into cable TV, and, in 1967, he formed Rogers Communication, a soon-to-be media giant. In 2000, he teamed up with Labatt Breweries to buy the Toronto Blue Jays baseball club, and, by 2003, he owned all of the team as well as the wonderful stadium they played in, the Skydome, which he promptly renamed the Rogers Centre.

Ted liked seeing his name on big-ticket items, and, in 2007, when he and wife Loretta donated $15 million to Ryerson University, it was on condition that the faculty of business be renamed the Ted Rogers School of Management. At only 75 years young, Ted Rogers passed away in 2008, and if he had lived another 10 years, there is little doubt that the City of Toronto would now be Rogers City.

We miss you Ted. Things are not the same with you gone.

DID YOU KNOW?

Pierre Salinger, press secretary to President John F. Kennedy, lived at 37 Lonsdale Road as a child, while author Farley Mowat lived down the road at 90 Lonsdale for a few years, and in the middle at 83 Lonsdale, whodunit author Joy Fielding practised her golf stroke and worked on her novels.

ABOUT THE ILLUSTRATORS

Roger Garcia

Roger Garcia is a self-taught artist with some formal training who specializes in cartooning and illustration. He is an immigrant from El Salvador, and during the last few years, his work has been primarily cartoons and editorial illustrations in pen and ink. Recently, he has started painting once more. Focusing on simplifying the human form, he uses a bright minimal palette and as few elements as possible. His work can be seen in newspapers, magazines, promo material and on www.rogergarcia.ca.

Peter Tyler

Peter is a graduate of the Vancouver Film School's Visual Art and Design and Classical animation programs. Though his ultimate passion is in filmmaking, he is also intent on developing his draftsmanship and storytelling, with the aim of using those skills in future filmic misadventures.

Patrick Hénaff

Born in France, Patrick Hénaff is mostly self-taught. He is a versatile artist who has explored a variety of media under many different influences. He now uses primarily pen and ink to draw, and then processes the images on computer. He is particularly interested in the narrative power of pictures and tries to use them as a way to tell stories.

Roly Wood

Roly has worked in Toronto as a freelance illustrator and was also employed in the graphic design department of a landscape architecture firm. In 2004, he wrote and illustrated a historical comic book set in Lang Pioneer Village near Peterborough, Ontario. To see more of Roly's work, visit www.rolywood.com.

Pat Bidwell

Pat has always had a passion for drawing and art. Initially self-taught, Pat completed art studies in visual communication in 1986. Over the years, he has worked both locally and internationally as an illustrator/product designer and graphic designer, collecting many awards for excellence along the way. When not at the drawing board, Pat pursues other interests solo and/or with his wife, Lisa.

ABOUT THE AUTHOR

Alan Jackson

Alan Jackson believes that, in the twine of life, there are two special genes unique to humankind—hope and humour—and he thinks we should all turn to the funny side of life in the face of adversity. He must have quite the sense of humour, then, since he's been struck by lightning five times!

Alan is a prolific writer of nonfiction and a creator of worlds in the fiction realm. For children mostly, because they have imaginations unconstrained by reality. Can pigs fly? No, but in one of his books, a pig talks, plots and saves mankind from becoming the bottom link of the food chain.

Alan lives in Toronto with a wife named M and a squirrel called Mommy. He is the author of various nonfiction titles, including *Weird Canadian Weather*, *Weird Ontario Weather* and *Weird Ontario Laws* also from Blue Bike Books.